AMERICAN HERITAGE

June, 1970 · Volume XXI, Number 4

This being June, a month of marriage and romance, we bring our readers some honeymooners. They regard each other fondly, as newlyweds are supposed to, and they make a handsome pair, despite the photographer's fraudulent backdrop. The place is Leavenworth, Kansas, and the couple, of all people, are William Frederick and Louisa (Frederici) Cody, who were married in St. Louis on March 6, 1866, and then moved out to Kansas. There young Cody, who had already served the Army as a scout, would gain fame killing buffalo in vast numbers to feed the construction gangs of the Kansas-Pacific Railroad. His work would win him the unforgettable nickname of Buffalo Bill, to be celebrated for years in dime novels, on the stage, and in the famous Wild West shows in which he forever played himself. Cody was a real frontier hero, a dead shot who duelled with the notorious Yellow Hand, a scout who his commandant swore could see better than a man with field glasses. He was also a great ham, an exaggerator, and a man who could barely read or sign his own name. The good and bad merge into a great figure who departed us at seventy, still full of energy and joy in life, in 1917. Louisa lived four more years and then joined him in a grave atop Lookout Mountain, near Golden, Colorado. The remarkable Leavenworth photographer who took the picture, E. E. Henry, is the subject of an article in this issue, beginning on page 16.

AMERICAN HERITAGE

The Magazine of History

SENIOR EDITOR
Bruce Catton

EDITOR
Oliver Jensen

ARTICLES EDITOR
E. M. Halliday

ASSOCIATE EDITORS
Nat Brandt   Barbara Klaw

ART DIRECTOR
Chester Prosinski

COPY EDITOR: Carol Angell

ASSOCIATE COPY EDITOR: Joyce O'Connor

ASSISTANT EDITORS
Jessica Bourgeois   Mary Dawn Earley
Carla Davidson   Constance M. Turnbull

CONSULTING EDITOR: Joan Paterson Kerr

CONSERVATION EDITOR
Anthony Wolff

ASSOCIATE CONSERVATION EDITOR
Elizabeth N. Layne

CONTRIBUTING EDITOR
Robert C. Alberts

PUBLISHER: Paul Gottlieb

ADVISORY BOARD
Allan Nevins, *Chairman*
Carl Carmer   Louis C. Jones
Gerald Carson   Alvin M. Josephy, Jr.
Marshall B. Davidson   Howard H. Peckham
John A. Garraty   Francis S. Ronalds
Eric F. Goldman   S. K. Stevens

American Heritage Publishing Co., Inc.

PRESIDENT
James Parton

CHAIRMAN, EDITORIAL COMMITTEE
Joseph J. Thorndike

MANAGING DIRECTOR, BOOK DIVISION
Richard M. Ketchum

EDITORIAL ART DIRECTOR
Murray Belsky

AMERICAN HERITAGE is published every two months by American Heritage Publishing Co., Inc.; editorial and executive offices, 551 Fifth Avenue, New York, N.Y. 10017. Treasurer, George W. Breitkreuz; Secretary, John C. Taylor III. Correspondence about subscriptions should be sent to American Heritage Subscription Office, 383 West Center Street, Marion, Ohio 43302. Single copies: $5.00. Annual subscriptions: $20.00 in U.S. and Canada; $21.00 elsewhere. An annual Index is published each spring, priced at $1.00. AMERICAN HERITAGE will consider but assumes no responsibility for unsolicited materials. Title registered U.S. Patent Office. Second-class postage paid at New York, N.Y., and at additional mailing offices.

Sponsored by
American Association for State & Local History · Society of American Historians

CONTENTS *June, 1970* · *Volume XXI, Number 4*

COVER: There are two schools of thought on General George Custer, and there probably always will be. Some see him as a great American hero, others as a great show-off; and there is much in the record to support both views. This portrait by Leonard Baskin, showing perhaps the Byronic picture Custer had of himself, is from a stunning little book newly published by the National Park Service (see pages 101–3). Less conspicuously, Custer also appears in a surprise picture on page 24. *Back Cover:* This French poster from the turn of the century extolls the virtues of the new Kodak Brownie, which, in theory at least, made everyone a potential portraitist. Even a child can take good pictures with a Brownie, exclaims the French tag line.

For His Was the Kingdom, and

On a green island in the cold waters of Lake Michigan, James Jesse Strang became the crowned, polygamous ruler of a Mormon "empire"

In the fall of 1846 a short man with a great reddish-brown beard walked into the phrenology parlor of Fowler and Wells at 131 Nassau Street, New York City, to purchase a phrenological examination. He was barely five feet three and of slight build, but his full auburn beard, his curiously bulging forehead, and his intense, deeply set dark eyes gave him a vividness and dramatic presence that compensated, along with his black stovepipe hat, for his short stature. After the report of the examination was written by Samuel R. Wells, the short man read it with satisfaction and left.

A trip to the phrenology parlor was hardly a rare occurrence in mid-nineteenth-century America. Nor was it even highly unusual that the short man in the stovepipe hat later published his nearly two-thousand-word phrenological description on the first page of a newspaper he edited. (Walt Whitman was so taken by the report Fowler and Wells wrote on *him* that he had it bound into early copies of *Leaves of Grass*.) But this particular visit to the phrenologist is of some interest because the man in the stovepipe hat was no ordinary person—as the phrenologist himself seemed to realize, even though his subject's name, James J. Strang, meant nothing to him.

The report said, for example, "You are quite radical in your notions," which is not a bad characterization of a man who convinced thousands of Mormons that an angel had designated him to succeed Joseph Smith as leader of the Church of Jesus Christ of Latter-day Saints. The phrenologist also credited him with "versatility of talent, which enables you to attend to a variety of things. . . ." Again, an apt comment on a man who besides serving as a state legislator was acknowledged as a full-fledged prophet to whom God had entrusted a major portion of the Bible, lost since the Babylonian captivity of the Jews in 597 B.C., and who was also an instinctive linguist who translated the ancient Oriental language in which the Biblical fragment was written, even though he had never studied any language but English. And certainly not the least of this versatile man's achievements was to have become a king whose kingdom lay within the United States and whose loyal subjects numbered in the thousands.

The learned phrenologist also said of him, "You are fond of variety and change," as he indeed was. At the time of his death he had five wives, the oldest forty-three, the youngest eighteen. Not only had they borne him ten children, most of whom lived with him and his four youngest wives in the royal palace, a solidly constructed log house in northern Michigan, but when he died each of the four youngest wives was with child. As Professor Wells perceptively remarked after carefully feeling and measuring the long narrow skull of James Jesse Strang with its bulging forehead, "You are fond of children, warm-hearted and ardent, and fond of home."

Beneath Strang's phrenological bumps pulsed a dream of personal glory that came true—though not as luxuriously as in a contemporary painting, here superimposed, of him and a few of his wives.

4   *By* ROBERT P. WEEKS

the Power, and the Glory...Briefly

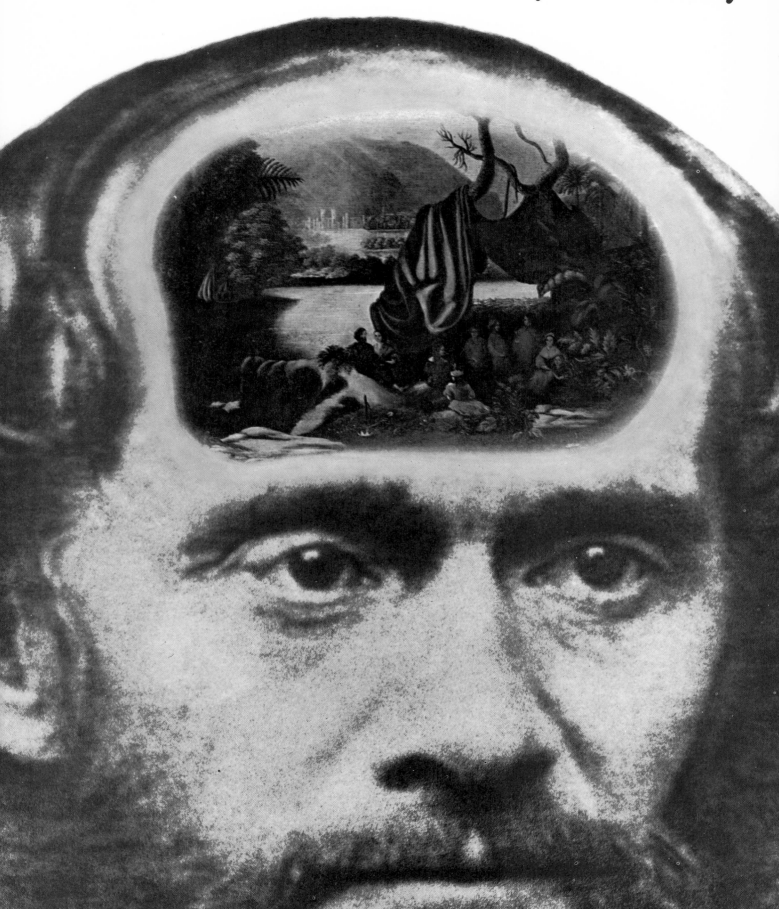

After Joseph Smith's death in 1844, Strang and Brigham Young were top contenders to lead the Mormon Church. The stability and stamina that made Young triumph are perhaps hinted at in this portrait of him and his second wife, Mary Ann Angell, with their six children. Her predecessor had died; after her were to come twenty-six additional wives and scores of children before Young died in 1877.

The professor erred, as a matter of fact, in only one observation he made; but admittedly it was a major error. He wrote: "Should you undertake to play the hypocrite, 'lay low and keep dark,' you would very soon expose yourself in some way, for you have not tact and cunning enough to enable you to carry it out into any great speculation or enterprise." That one sentence is enough to repudiate forever the science of phrenology, for James J. Strang's supply of tact and cunning was truly extraordinary. And how could anyone deny that creating a kingdom within the United States qualifies as a "great speculation or enterprise"? To have reigned even as briefly as a half dozen years was an achievement; for kings, as one historian drily summed it up, have never done well in the United States.

Strang was able to pull this off because he brought to the task of creating a kingdom not only tact and cunning but a rare mixture of idealism and deceit, saintly asceticism and sexual appetite, backwoods utopianism and Napoleonic authoritarianism. His followers, mostly a ragtag collection of poor, uneducated pioneers, were not too blinded by ignorance and superstition to perceive both sides of his character. The trouble was that few of them could see both sides simultaneously. As a result, during his career as prophet and king, at any given time most of his followers saw him as not merely godly but godlike, the prophet who would lead them to Zion. But there were always others, a minority who saw him as a cynical opportunist—eloquent, yes, but lascivious and dictatorial.

Strang's origins were far from regal. He was born on a small farm near the town of Scipio in Cayuga County, New York, in 1813. It was a time of deep religious ferment, and upstate New York seemed to have more than its share of strange religious goings-on. For example, when Strang was ten years old, an angel with the odd name of Moroni allegedly appeared in the bedroom of a farmhouse in the next county to tell a seventeen-year-old farm boy that God had written a new Bible on golden plates and buried them in a nearby hill. Young Joseph Smith dug up the plates; then, with the help of two magical stones provided by Moroni, he translated them as *The Book of Mormon* and became the founder of the Church of Latter-day Saints.

Even though Strang some twenty years later was to be a strong contender to succeed Smith as head of the Mormon Church, as a boy he was unaware of Smith, Moroni, and the plates. Indeed, Strang's youthful religious development moved from agnosticism to skepticism. As he grew into adulthood in the 1830's, he turned to the rationalism of thinkers like Tom Paine and the Comte de Volney. Upon completion of his meager formal education, Strang read law; he was admitted to the Chautauqua County bar in 1836. He did a stint as a small-town postmaster and won admiration for his wit and eloquence as a debater.

But beneath this rather ordinary surface strange currents stirred. In his diary on his nineteenth birthday, March 21, 1832, Strang wrote: "I am 19 years old and am yet no more than a common farmer. 'Tis too bad. I ought to have been a member of the Assembly or a Brigadier General before this time if I am ever to rival *Cesar or Napoleon* which I have *sworn to*." (The five underscored words were written in a cipher of Strang's invention that was not decoded until a few years ago.)

Later that spring he confided to his diary in his private cipher: "I have spent the day in trying to contrive some plan of obtaining in marriage the heir to the English Crown." (The lady would have been the future Queen Victoria, then twelve.) If a nineteen-year-old New York farm boy is to become a king, he obviously needs to give it quite a bit of thought. And James Jesse Strang gave it a great deal. His preoccupation with power appears again and again in his youthful diary. On New Year's Day, 1835, for example, he wrote of those who had "died in obscurity" the previous year. Then Strang added fervently: "Curse me eternally if that be my fate."

Yet nothing he did in the next half dozen years gave promise of escape from such a fate: he married a Baptist preacher's daughter, served as a temperance lecturer, and became a small-town weekly newspaper editor. But when he migrated to Burlington, Wisconsin, with his wife and child in the summer of 1843, he had without knowing it taken a major step toward his royal destiny.

In Burlington, Strang took up for the first time the practice of law. During his first winter in the territory, he attended a Mormon meeting to hear an apostle of Joseph Smith's known as the Wild Ram of the Mountains. Strang had never been susceptible to the theatricality of evangelical preachers. In fact, he had described himself in his diary as "a cool Philosopher." But perhaps when he saw how the Wild Ram could shake the windowpanes and move his listeners to religious ecstasy, he was envious. We have no record of his feelings, but we know he was sufficiently interested in Mormonism to journey some two hundred miles to the south, to Nauvoo, Illinois, where after talking with Joseph Smith he was baptized a Mormon.

As he baptized Strang, the Prophet is reported to have said: "Thou shalt hold the Keys of the Melchizedek priesthood, shalt walk with Moses, Enoch, and Elijah, and shalt talk with God face to face." It was not quite like marrying the heir to the British throne, but it had possibilities. Especially in 1844; for Illinois seethed with political intrigue and violent anti-Mormon feeling. Clearly, the sect could not last much longer in Nauvoo. When Strang proposed to Joseph Smith and his brother Hyrum that he found a Mormon colony near Burlington, Wisconsin, they made him an elder of the church and urged him to report on the possibilities to the north.

Strang's report from Burlington came too late for Joseph Smith to do much about it. On June 27, a few days after receiving it, Joseph and Hyrum were killed by a mob in Carthage, Illinois. Smith had been such a colorful, powerful leader that to many his death meant the end of Mormonism. In the New York *Herald*'s obituary James Gordon Bennett wrote, "The death of the modern Mahomet will seal the fate of Mormonism. They cannot get another Joe Smith. The holy city must tumble into ruins, and the 'latter day saints' have indeed come to the latter day."

To Bennett's credit he revised this judgment two days later: "Instead of sealing the fate of Mormonism, we are now rather inclined to believe that this revolting transaction may give only additional and increased strength to that sect." But the immediate future of the church was extremely dark. As the twelve apostles who ruled the church under Smith assembled in Nauvoo, they were in

CONTINUED ON PAGE 78

James Jesse Strang about 1854. The blow-up on page 5 is from the same daguerreotype.

Strang's first "plural" wife, Elvira, in male attire pending angelic word of her legality

7

"AN AGREABLE VOYAGE"

Helen, Countess of Selkirk

The village of Kirkcudbright, Scotland, as it looked when Jones landed

On the morning of April 23, 1778, the Countess of Selkirk, granddaughter to the Earl of Haddington and wife of the fourth Earl of Selkirk, was lingering over breakfast in the Selkirk mansion on St. Mary's Isle—actually a small peninsula in Kirkcudbright Bay on the Scottish coast. She had no idea that she was presently to earn a colorful place in the history of the American Revolution. Had she known this she probably would not have been pleased; for although her husband the Earl disapproved of King George's war against the colonists, she felt little doubt that they were generally uncouth people unfit to associate with nobility. The Countess, who was soon to give birth to a child, had better things to think about than war. Neither she nor proper old Daniel, the butler, who busied himself clearing away the breakfast silver, was aware that America's first and only invasion of England had taken place this morning, just twenty miles away. Daniel poured the Countess a bit more tea from her shiny silver teapot. Perhaps he wondered when the Earl would return home from Buxton in Derbyshire. . . .

Two weeks earlier, on April 9, 1778, a man with considerably more ambition than old Daniel had set sail from Brest, France, in command of an eighteen-gun sloop of war, the U.S.S. *Ranger*. It was now almost thirty-one years since the *Ranger*'s captain had been born in a stone cottage at Arbigland in the parish of Kirkbean, less than thirty-five miles from the Selkirk mansion, and christened John Paul, after his father. And it had been over six years since he had last seen his Scottish homeland.

By MARK HALLIDAY

In which John Jones, né Paul, invades both England and Scotland, despoils

a countess, and defeats a British sloop—all in less than forty-eight hours

by to attempt the kidnapping of the local peer, the Earl of Selkirk

John Paul Jones in 1776

At that time young John Paul had already put in four years as master of a brig in the West Indies trade. He had also been in trouble. A carpenter whom he had flogged for disrespectful conduct later died of fever, and John Paul was accused of having caused the man's demise. The young captain cleared himself of the charge but carried away from the episode a dislike for the Scottish authorities who had beleaguered him. Throughout his career John Paul was to mystify people by being alternately, or even simultaneously, gentle and harsh. The log of a later command records that one Midshipman Potter was "ordered in irons by the Capt. for a thermometer being broke in his Cabbin." Yet when the *Ranger* was in France "the Capt." had paid advance wages with his own money and had gone out of his way

to acquire plenty of brandy to raise the men's spirits. His habitual concern for his sailors' welfare throws doubt on the charge that he was tyrannical; but there can be no doubt that this captain was highly temperamental.

A year after John Paul extricated himself from the affair of the carpenter, in 1773, he got into a brawl with mutineers and ended it by killing their leader with his sword. This incident led him to adopt a pseudonym and flee the threat of another murder trial, arriving in Virginia in 1774 to find a new career. His new last name was to be Jones, and along with this name he adopted a brand-new nation. Both John Paul Jones and America were starting out afresh, and each was to be of great service to the other. In the summer of 1775 Jones went

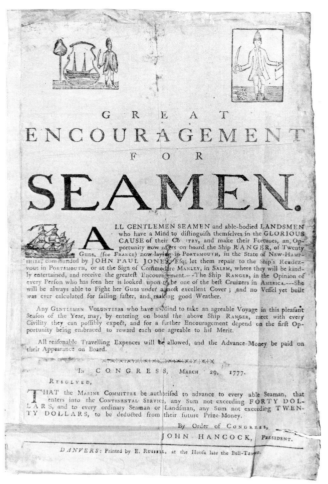

The recruiting poster issued by the Continental Congress in 1777 to lure a crew for Jones's voyage on the Ranger *somewhat oversold the "agreable" aspects, resulting in later discontent.*

to Philadelphia unemployed; by December he had impressed enough congressmen with his sea experience to be commissioned as a first lieutenant in the fledgling United States Navy.

But now, in 1778, Captain Jones had not forgotten his life as John Paul. The contours of the Scottish coasts that had posed his first problems of navigation were still clear in his memory, and he was determined to use his knowledge in fulfilling the *Ranger*'s mission. He could hardly have felt less fettered by his orders. The American representatives in Paris had freed him to proceed "in the manner you shall judge best for distressing the Enemies of the United States, by sea or otherwise, consistent with the laws of war." In 1778 the American Navy was struggling to become a moderately effective fighting force; it boasted only a few frigates to challenge the huge and renowned Royal Navy. With such limited striking capacity, Captain Jones had always argued, the Navy's

proper role was not to exchange broadsides with bigger British ships; nor was it merely to harass enemy supply vessels. Instead the Navy should do what privateers seeking booty would never do: prevent England from bringing her full weight to bear on the seas by hitting her at home. As he directed the *Ranger* northward between Ireland and Wales, Jones was eager to make the first trial of this strategy.

In addition, he hoped to find some way of pressuring the British government into recognizing the rights of American seamen taken prisoner. So far the enemy, while acknowledging that Washington's soldiers were part of a legitimate army, had insisted on calling all American ships privateers and jailing our Navy men as sea bandits. Such a policy was bound to rankle in the mind of a man whose future depended on whether or not the Continental Navy would win respect on the seas. "This circumstance more than any other," he wrote, "rendered me the avowed enemy of Great Britain." Thus the mission of the *Ranger* was twofold: to interfere with the British war effort at its source, and to promote the exchange of American naval prisoners.

Captain Jones's great expectations were limited, however, by his dissatisfaction with his ship and her crew. From Brest he had written apologetically to the French Minister of Marine: "I am, sir, ambitious of being employed in active and enterprising services; but my ship is too small a force and does not sail as fast as I could wish." Indeed, although the *Ranger* was a new vessel, she had plenty of defects. For one thing, her masts were too big, having been cut for a much larger warship; this made her top-heavy, so that she would heel far over on her side even in mild winds. At Brest, Jones had ordered extensive improvements of the sloop's poorly made sails, and the mainmast and mizzen had been moved farther aft to adjust her balance; but the fact remained that the *Ranger* was not the formidable warship Jones felt he deserved.

Nor did her officers measure up to the captain's standards. All were men of Portsmouth, New Hampshire, where the *Ranger* had been built, and Jones had had very little voice in their selection. None of them had served in the Continental Navy before; they had made their reputations in the merchant marine, not in battle. The precise naval discipline that Jones sought to impose seemed silly and undemocratic to them, and the captain's assistants were even less enamored of him than he was of them. First Lieutenant Simpson was nine years older than Jones, Second Lieutenant Hall was five years older; they were not accustomed to obeying a younger man, especially one who stood only 5 feet 5 inches tall. These rough-hewn fellows found Jones's fine manners offensive and his Scottish background suspicious.

The crew shared the attitudes of their lieutenants, and

throughout their service on the *Ranger* they were inclined to regard Simpson, a man of loudly voiced opinions, as their rightful leader, and Jones as an interloper. Simpson was quite willing to encourage this feeling. Finally, every man on board was there above all for prize money, not for military service. The poster printed to invite their enlistment had offered them opportunities "to distinguish themselves in the GLORIOUS CAUSE of their COUNTRY, and make their Fortunes"—but it soon became clear that most of them had dismissed the first phrase as mere rhetoric. Nor were they eager to court danger in their pursuit of profit; they had been told that the *Ranger*'s mission was to be "an agreable Voyage in this pleasant Season of the Year."

Such were the expectations of the men handling Jones's imperfect 110-foot sloop of war as she entered the Irish Sea. They were only temporarily mollified when they made a prize of the *Lord Chatham*, an Irish merchant ship heading for Dublin, and sent her back to Brest under a prize crew. They performed smartly enough in the next few days as the *Ranger* sank two supply vessels and frightened off two small armed ships. Then, on the morning of Monday, April 20, Jones sighted an enemy warship at anchor in the harbor of Belfast Lough. A short while later four astonished Irish fishermen in a small boat were captured by the *Ranger* when they passed too close to the harmless-looking ship —for the *Ranger* was disguised as a merchantman, with red cloth draped over her gunports and a Dutch pennant and British jack flying from her masthead. When ques-

CONTINUED ON PAGE 70

BY EDWARD MORAN; U.S. NAVAL ACADEMY, ANNAPOLIS

When the Ranger *sailed into Quiberon Bay, France, on February 13, 1778, it was one of the great moments of American naval history: to signal the first recognition of the Stars and Stripes by a foreign power, the entire French fleet fired a nine-gun salute.*

John A. Garraty interviews Alfred Kazin

A Century of American Realism

Mark Twain

Henry James

William Dean Howells

Professor John A. Garraty of Columbia University is the author of a collection of interviews with eminent American scholars, Interpreting American History: Conversations with Historians, *just published by Macmillan. To give an added dimension to this absorbing series of discussions, he arranged an interview with a distinguished literary critic, Alfred Kazin. In addition to several works of criticism, including his influential* On Native Grounds: An Interpretation of Modern American Prose Literature (*1942*), *Mr. Kazin has edited the works of such writers as F. Scott Fitzgerald and Theodore Dreiser; he also is the author of two autobiographical volumes,* A Walker in the City (*1951*) *and* Starting Out in the Thirties (*1965*). *The following interview has been slightly abridged.*—The Editors

PROFESSOR GARRATY: *Professor Kazin, why do you choose as the topic for our discussion "a century" of realism in the American novel, rather than, say, one hundred and fifty or even two hundred years?*

PROFESSOR KAZIN: The American novel, as a realistic form, began just about one hundred years ago when men like Henry James and William Dean Howells, who were very much influenced by European novelists, suddenly began to write realistically about American society. The novel as a form really began around that time. I don't mean that there weren't novels before, but they were really what used to be called the "romance." Melville, Cooper, and Hawthorne were romanticists, properly speaking.

The major difference between James and Howells, on the one hand, and people like Hawthorne and Cooper and Poe is, first of all, that James and Howells thought that the novel was the greatest possible literary form. They were full of admiration for the great European novelists, especially Balzac (the master of them all), but also Tolstoy and Dostoevsky, and they believed that modern society in all its aspects was the proper subject of the writer. The word "realism," though it can be very confusing, had to do with this concern for reality in fiction. James and Howells didn't like to use the word. Only late in his career did Howells speak of the necessity of being a realist, and James hardly ever did. But they were both thinking of reality in this sense of the word, and today Saul Bellow, Norman Mailer, James Jones, Louis Auchincloss, and how many other depicters of modern American society have the same point of view. But in the romantic fiction that was published before the Civil War—in Poe's hallucinated stories, in Hawthorne's guilt-ridden, fear-filled characters, and of course in Melville's great apocalyptic novel *Moby Dick*, the approach is quite different. One gets the lonely individual, very much concerned with his physical fate, in a world ridden by demons and ghosts and ancestral symbols, as in Hawthorne, or with religious problems, as in Melville.

Only with James and Howells, roughly a century ago, did this marvelous sense of the world as a place that can be accepted for itself alone begin to appear.

With the new taste for realism in literature came an appreciation of realism in painting and drawing. It is no accident that the art which Henry James all his life loved more than any other was painting. It was allied also to the novelists' sense that Europe provided the natural environment for a writer. The American writer who went abroad came to see himself as a detached spectator of American life. When he came back, he was changed.

The new realism was allied also to the influence of magazines. Writers like Poe and Hawthorne had made a living, if you can call it a living, by writing for magazines, and in fact much of their best work was in the form of short fiction. But suddenly magazines like the *Atlantic Monthly*, which had been founded before the Civil War, became extraordinarily hospitable to a new kind of realistic short story. There was a very clear-cut beginning to this trend. It began when William Dean Howells became assistant editor of the *Atlantic* and met Henry James. They discovered how much they had in common, and they discovered, too, that they could take on the whole of American society as a literary project. They felt themselves part of a movement.

Another aspect of realism was that for the first time a certain kind of American woman became the principal character in novels. *Daisy Miller* [1879] depicted a type of woman who hadn't appeared in American fiction, or in American life, before. Almost a century later, when the freedom and the vitality of women clearly exemplify what has happened to American society, it's a fact of some interest to look back and realize that James's awareness of this "new" woman is pretty much what distinguishes him as a novelist. When James saw the young American girl sitting on the piazza of the Grand Union Hotel in Saratoga Springs, surrounded by her parents and possible suitors, she stood out for the same reason that she stood out for Henry Adams: in a society full of rather tiresome money-getters, she was a symbol of culture and refinement and the only person who seemed to be interested in beauty per se. This is what Henry Adams meant when he said in his *Education* that he never knew an American woman who wasn't better than her husband. Winslow Homer expressed this point of view in a different medium in his paintings of the young American girls walking in their flowing summer gowns on the cliffs of Newport, holding up their parasols as feminine insignia. Of course, the other side of this is that the audience for the novels of James and Howells and other novelists was very much an audience of women. This is still true, to my knowledge. I almost never see a man carrying a book unless it is a textbook or income-tax guide, whereas women still do carry novels and best sellers. The feminization of culture seemed to James of very great importance. Women were his readers; women were his main characters; women were the principal new form which attracted the interest of writers like Howells and James and even Mark Twain, though what they did with women in their books was something else again.

The early realistic writers in America, despite their interest in women, displayed very little of the European realists' concern with sexuality in their books. What Henry Adams said about Henry James is in a sense true of all of them: James knew nothing about women except the outside. Of course, James never had a wife, but Howells and Twain were married, and they were nonetheless very careful not to touch on any vital aspect of human passion.

Isn't that related to the fact that American culture was really a subdivision of British culture, and that the period we're talking about was the height of the Victorian Age? Were English writers of stature dealing with sexuality at this time?

The so-called Victorian attitude toward sex was really a very temporary interlude in the English literary tradition of healthy licentiousness. The eighteenth-century English novelists were extremely frank and even bawdy in this respect, and even Dickens, when he came over here, made a point of shocking Americans by saying, for example, that he didn't want his sons to be virgins when they were married. The American attitude toward sexuality was peculiarly American in this period, because of the actual roughness of American society. The literary class was very genteel and very careful; I'm often fascinated by the self-conscious gentility of Howells and James and even of Mark Twain. All of them wrote exquisitely; they were all marvelous stylists. But they were all rather goody-goody when it came to literary culture. Their air of superior refinement was their way of getting away from the roughness of the American experience more than anything else. This was fundamental. The American novel today has certainly gone to the other extreme, but the early realists felt themselves to be a part of that small Brahmin class—even Mark Twain, the self-educated printer and frontiersman. And as a result, their work displays a certain tendency to elegance quite different from the aristocratic quality of English fiction in this period. Of course, the English had a much more complex society to describe. The American experience was peculiarly narrow in this sense. That was one of the reasons why James went to England, why he started writing novels about English society.

James and Howells—James particularly—considered Balzac simply *the* greatest novelist that Europe had ever produced. They felt he could create his splendid imaginative world only because of the great variety of classes in Europe and because of the conflict between the aristocracy and the emerging middle classes. They were trying to show that these class differences could in some way be suggested even in America. Since the whole epic of industrial capitalism dealt with the upward struggle of the middle classes—the effort described by Dickens in *Bleak House* and by Balzac in *Père Goriot*—James and Howells tried to find this in American life, too. It was far more difficult because there was less variety in America. When Howells tried to describe a Boston aristocrat in *The Rise of Silas Lapham*, he produced an elegant but pretty sterile character.

How did "naturalistic" writers like Theodore Dreiser, Stephen Crane, and Frank Norris differ from James and Howells and Twain? Did their work develop logically out of that of the older generation of realists?

Crane, Dreiser, and Norris were all born within a few months of each other, and two of them, Norris and Crane, died at a very early age. Crane and Dreiser fascinate me because they were both extremely gifted but nonetheless very different. Dreiser was clumsy and verbose, but he wrote very powerfully. Crane was one of the most amazing geniuses we've ever produced. The 1890's represent the great watershed of American history, not only in fiction but in politics—the beginning of open class struggles, of open polarization in American life. A cocky, disparaging attitude toward the bourgeois experience developed; the ethos of the middle class had been exploded. Many of the younger writers were much more cynical, much less hidebound by genteel conventions. Can you imagine Henry James going as a correspondent to the Greco-Turkish War as Crane did? Or having the kind of experience that Dreiser did when he was taken in by a prostitute in Evansville, Indiana, who happened to be his brother Paul's mistress? Or having the concern with money that Crane had all his life and that made Dreiser, as a young man, steal from the laundry for which he worked? The writers of the 1890's represented a tougher, harsher, crueler world. Take Crane's fascination with war. Everybody knows that he wrote *The Red Badge of Courage* before he ever saw a battle. Yet many Civil War veterans thought that he had been at Chancellorsville. Crane saw the life of America as war, the life of the world as war.

Crane was the son of a Methodist minister; he grew up in a religious, Christian home. His mother was a pillar of the Women's Christian Temperance Union. Yet, coming from this respectable, almost traditional kind of American background, Crane found himself always looking at things with a beady eye—finding objects of derision in American institutions. When he came to New York as a newspaper reporter and began to observe the misery and degradation of slum life, he was intoxicated by the literary possibilities of this kind of world. Compare Crane on

New York in the 1890's with what William Dean Howells was writing about the East Side! Howells was a very decent man. He was a utopian socialist. He was properly dismayed by the fate of Jewish immigrants living in East Side tenements. But he regarded this as something with which he had no personal relationship. He felt rather disgusted by the slum dwellers, although he rose above his disgust like a true gentleman. Crane, on the contrary, was delighted with the life of the Bowery. He was fascinated by what used to be called "fallen women"; he defended prostitutes who were being shaken down by the police so vigorously that the police wouldn't give him any peace. Unlike James and Howells, Dreiser and Crane both were seriously concerned with low life.

They also had very strong feelings about religion. Dreiser, the first important American writer who was not a Protestant, reacted bitterly against the Catholic Church in which he was raised. He hated orthodox religion and conventional morality. The literary historians make too much of what is called naturalism as a style. It was wholly a social-human question: these writers were a new class of people; they were at war with middle-class values. Crane lived with an extraordinarily vivid and courageous woman, Cora, who had kept a whorehouse in Jacksonville, Florida. They lived in England because they couldn't have that kind of relationship in the United States.

I know that Howells appreciated and aided some of the naturalist writers. What about Henry James?

Even Howells didn't like all of them. He was a very generous critic, a great supporter of all new fiction. But there were severe limitations to his appreciation. He thought *Maggie*, Stephen Crane's first book, wonderful, but he did not like *The Red Badge of Courage* for reasons I'm not sure I understand entirely. I think the fact that in *Maggie* the young girl becomes a prostitute and eventually commits suicide must have pleased his moral sense. But in *The Red Badge of Courage*, a masterpiece written in letters of fire, the underlying depiction of the violence of war apparently distressed Howells' peaceful soul.

Howells didn't like Dreiser at all. Despite his importance, Dreiser is still one of the most neglected figures in American literature. All sorts of literary professors are still afraid of him. But in his own time Dreiser was treated with the most incredible contempt and hostility by the literary establishment. They always, of course, complained about his bad writing, though they didn't seem to mind it when they read other things just as bad. In point of fact, it was his attitude toward society that they didn't like—his conviction that there wasn't, fundamentally, any real design to life.

James and Howells, after all, were profoundly ethical writers. At the end of James's novels there is always a

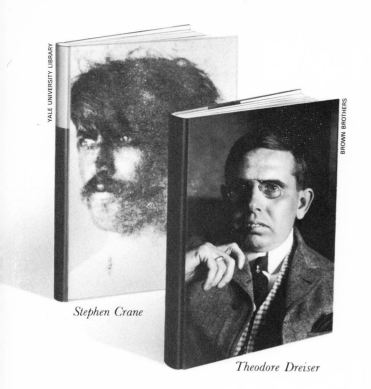

Stephen Crane

Theodore Dreiser

criminals, precisely because it was a way of shocking the people he'd lived with before. Nothing delighted him more than to feel he was a scapegrace, in some way a naughty fellow. But he wasn't warm. He didn't care a hang about Dora Clark, the famous prostitute he defended. He just hated the police and was outraged because he thought that they were being mean to her. He had no feeling of closeness to Bowery bums; he felt that these people were all helpless.

As we know from Crane's most famous story, one of the greatest stories in the world, "The Open Boat," he was interested in getting at the facts of experience. It is a description of what he went through in a dinghy after the *Commodore*, the ship he was taking from Florida, blew up in the water. Sitting in this dinghy, freezing and starving and expecting at any moment to be drowned, he observed everything with a cold, clear eye. That shocked readers, too; he was able to write about things with merciless detachment.

After all, that is what makes the novelist the novelist. No matter how warm he may feel about people, fundamentally he's a professional. The professional eye is an extraordinary thing in such writers; it gives them a kind of chilling expertise in describing things which would involve other people emotionally.

The difficulty with that statement to me is that it removes the writer from the society he's a part of.

I guess I didn't put that very clearly. Professionalism in any field has nothing to do with one's own emotions. Any historian who's studying a subject may be personally involved with it in terms of memory or sympathy, but he tries to get at the facts as far as he understands them. No one, to this day, has given us a better picture of the transformation of American life in the 1890's than Crane did, in *Maggie*, in *George's Mother*, and even in "The Open Boat," precisely because he saw clearly what was happening. To use a modern example, I happen to admire Norman Mailer's book on the Pentagon, *The Armies of the Night*, very much. I think it's the best thing that's been written about the political atmosphere in which we've been living since the Vietnam war started. His book seems to me a triumph of detachment and involvement at the same time.

Were all the early realists gifted with this combination of detachment and insight?

I think so. James and Howells in their earlier work show very clearly what a great age of confidence the 1870's and 1880's were for the people they were writing about: the northern middle classes who went to Saratoga and Newport and lived in the best of all possible worlds. Then, bit by bit, one sees in their work a growing anxiety. Howells became a socialist; he grew more and more

subtle victory for the human conscience. Goodness wins out, as in *The Wings of the Dove* or in *The Golden Bowl*. These books are, in a sense, religious allegories. But in Crane, and especially in Dreiser, there is a strong feeling that there is no design, no meaning. They keep themselves separate from anything they are describing. With them the human being is getting more and more difficult to reach and describe intimately; there are nothing like the marvelous close-ups that you get in James's novels. In Crane and Dreiser the world is pretty much a cold world. People are described as if they are far off. This coldness toward the world, toward human beings, becomes the limiting fact in American fiction later on.

How can this be reconciled with what you said about Crane's warmth, his reaction to poverty and vice on the Bowery?

I didn't say he was warm, I said he was interested. When I spoke of distance in the fiction of Crane and Dreiser, I meant their sense that what they were writing about was far removed from them. We can see the same thing in our own lives. We write about politics and power and the people around us, but we feel ourselves to be engulfed by too many people, too many problems, too many pressures. We are more detached; the world's become more complex, more overwhelming. Crane was interested in writing about the Bowery for literary and artistic reasons. He regarded the people on the Bowery as aesthetic facts. He was fascinated by the new opportunity, the new material he found there. His concern for prostitutes reflected only his rejection of his father's morality. That's why he liked being a police reporter. He liked to hobnob with

CONTINUED ON PAGE 86

15

THE PAST SPRINGS

OUT OF A PICTURE

Photographs by
E. E. HENRY *and* HARRISON PUTNEY,

from the collection of
DAVID R. PHILLIPS

In the next few pages we take our readers on what we regard as a magical journey into the past. It begins at the right with one of the two frames of a stereopticon view, reproduced in its exact original size. The scene is a railway station at Leavenworth, Kansas, in 1867, and it is scarcely prepossessing. Even the planting of two girls in the foreground (an old ploy of our esteemed contemporary the *National Geographic*) does little for the photograph. But that is the heart of the matter. Life lurks within the picture, waiting to be released. Turn the page and see what happens when one part of it is enlarged. Then open the double fold-out and look at a detail of that enlargement spread over four of our pages. Suddenly there is no end to what can be seen; you are right there, in a suspended moment, almost jostling against the everyday life of over a century ago.

Uncounted thousands of such photographs, some better, some worse, were produced all over the country in the nineteenth century, and a great many of them survive—but as prints. Only a handful of the old glass-plate negatives are to be found, and they alone make possible (when they are sharp) such enlargements as these. Finding them and working with them is the fascinating avocation of David R. Phillips, of Chicago, a free-lance photographer and master darkroom technician who has assembled several excellent glass-plate collections. Using special light sources and a new breed of lenses, Phillips makes a fine art of the business of bringing to vivid life minute and unsuspected details.

His searches took Phillips to Leavenworth not long ago, and there he acquired thirteen tons of plates covering the town, its people, and its events from 1855 to 1920. Most of the photographs in this treasure house of middle-western history were the product of E. E. (for Ebenezer Elijah) Henry and his stepson Harrison Putney. (Henry appears at left in the picture opposite, taken about 1867 when he was forty, together with a friend, Dr. Elbee.) They spent their lives running a photographic business in Leavenworth, Henry dying in 1917 at ninety, and Putney in 1950 at eighty-six. They witnessed the rise of a frontier post on the Missouri River into a big town that called itself, in the modest manner of the time, the Queen City of the West; it was, in fact, the largest city between St. Louis and San Francisco. They also saw it decline into a small town built around the fort and prison. But meanwhile, as their plates assert, much life had been lived in Leavenworth.

This is Leavenworth, Kansas, in 1867, in a stereopticon view looking past the railroad station toward the Missouri. Freight and passenger cars line the tracks. Men are loading and unloading supplies for the Santa Fe and Oregon trails, both of which passed close by the fast-growing town. Between 1855 and 1861, for example, population increased from 270 to 8,000; it was the biggest city in Kansas and had five railroad lines by 1872. But the big lines bypassed Leavenworth eventually, and the place diminished in importance. The tracks are still there, carrying freight only; the depot is gone.

*Turn the page. . .
Then open the fold-out*

Behind the fence and its odd stile stands Syracuse House, one of the fine buildings among the officers' quarters at Fort Leavenworth. That is all one sees in the original size of the photograph, but let us look at right into the porch through David Phillips' enlarger. Peering out at us is General George Armstrong Custer, to the left, with his wife, a maid, and their baby. It has to be either 1869 or 1870, years when Custer was thirty and thirty-one, and posted to Leavenworth. (See also cover and pages 101–103.) The eight-thousand-acre fort housed many famous Indian fighters and scouts, and Henry kept busy photographing passing celebrities like Wild Bill Hickok. The fort became known as the Mother-in-Law of the Army, because so many Leavenworth girls married its soldiers. General Grant was there on several occasions and was recorded in the rather unusual white-haired portrait opposite, taken at fifty-nine in 1881. One of the most striking of these pictures is at far right center; it shows the eight-year-old son of Captain Arthur MacArthur all dressed up for a fancy-dress ball in the 1800's. The boy's name was Douglas.

James Butler "Wild Bill" Hickok

An Army captain's son

General Ulysses S. Grant

Above is a routine view of Fifth Street in Leavenworth looking north from the intersection with Shawnee, a business area, shot at some odd hour when few people were about. At left, Phillips has taken a minute segment of the photograph and enlarged it to make a rather interesting composition.

In similar fashion, the picture below contains the detail shown as a blowup on the opposite page—although it is easier to find than the wooden Indian in the other scene. The sporty drugstore loiterer was photographed by Henry from the intersection of Shawnee and Fourth streets.

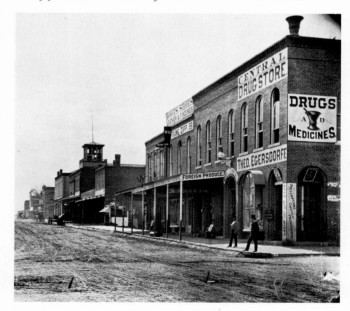

Henry Adams

IN
SEARCH
OF
INNOCENCE

John LaFarge

By LOUIS AUCHINCLOSS

When Marian Hooper Adams took her fatal dose of potassium cyanide on December 6, 1885, she almost smashed the life out of her husband as well. Suicide makes a clean sweep of the past and present; worst of all, it repudiates love. Until that day Henry Adams might have reasonably considered that his life was successful. He had not, to be sure, been President of the United States, like his grandfather and great-grandfather, or minister to England, like his father, but he had been a brilliant and popular teacher of medieval history at Harvard, a successful editor of the *North American Review*, a noted biographer and essayist, and he was in process of completing his twelve-volume history of the Jefferson and Madison administrations, which even such a self-deprecator as he himself must have suspected would one day be a classic. But above all this, far above, he had believed that he and his wife were happy.

Recovering from the first shock, he took a trip to Japan with his friend John LaFarge. Then he went back to Washington and worked for three laborious years to finish his history and prepare it for the press. After that, at last, he was free. He had neither child nor job, and his means were ample. In August of 1890 he and LaFarge sailed again from San Francisco for a voyage of indefinite duration to the South Seas. Many writers have speculated on why he went. Edward Chalfant, who in my opinion is the scholar closest to the secrets of Adams' personality, told me that he had once made a list of seventeen possible motives. Suffice it to say that Adams had reached the end of one life and was wondering if another existed.

LaFarge was the perfect travelling companion. Ernest Samuels has described him as an original genius with a Faustian nature who maintained a large, devoutly Catholic family in Newport while he kept bachelor's hall in New York. He was delighted to explore the Pacific at Adams' expense, leaving family and creditors behind. A master in oils and water colors, he could also talk and write exuberantly on all the subjects that he reproduced.

The Pacific opened up a new dimension of color. LaFarge's journal is a hymn to the sea and air. He taught Adams to observe the exquisite clearness of the butterfly blue of the sky, laid on between clouds and shading down to a white faintness in the distance where the haze of ocean covered up the turquoise. He made him peer down into the water, framed in the opening of a ship's gangway, and see how the sapphire blue seemed to pour from it. He pointed out the varieties of pink and lilac and purple and rose in the clouds at sunset. Adams never learned to be more than an amateur painter, but his vision was immensely sharpened.

They went first to Oahu, where they made the discovery which every other island was to confirm: that the charm of the Pacific declined in exact proportion to the penetration of the white man. It was not until October, when they landed on Upolu in the Samoas, that

The movement and colors of Samoan life fascinated John LaFarge, as in this water color he painted of natives beaching an outrigger.

they came in touch with a culture that was still largely unspoiled. The natives, grave and courteous, greeted them benevolently and made them feel immediately at home. They drank the ceremonial kava, muddy water mixed with grated root, which left a persistent little aftertaste that no amount of coconut milk could quite wash away, and they watched the siva, a dance performed by girls naked to the waist, their dark skins shining with coconut oil, seated cross-legged with garlands of green leaves around their heads and loins. The girls chanted as they swayed and stretched out their arms in all directions; they might have come out of the nearby sea. LaFarge's spectacles quivered with emotion, but Adams was able to assure his correspondent Elizabeth Cameron that nothing in the song or dance suggested the least impropriety. Again and again he was to comment on such evidences of Rousseauistic innocence.

Samoa was ruled by Malietoa, the puppet king of the Western nations' consuls, but Mataafa, the deposed monarch, still held the loyalty of most of the population. Adams and LaFarge, scrupulously neutral, called on both and learned a concept of aristocracy beside which Adams felt like "the son of a camel driver degraded to the position of stable boy in Spokane West Centre." For the real art of the Samoans was social. Even the breeding among the chiefs was systematic. They selected their wives for strength and form, with the result that the principal families enjoyed a physical as well as a social

superiority. Yet at the same time Adams observed that the society was basically communistic. All of the presents that he and LaFarge lavishly handed out to their hosts—umbrellas, silk scarfs, gowns, cigars—were soon seen parading about the villages on strangers. Every chief was basically a poor man because he was obliged to share what he had.

In Apia the travellers found the first corrosive effects of European influence. In the big siva organized in their honor by the American consul, the girls deferred to missionary prejudices by wearing banana leaves over their breasts. Adams was at once reminded of the world and the devil. In 1970 we are amused at his surprise that the Polynesian standard of female beauty should be more in the body than the face, but we must remember that in 1890 the face was all that the American woman exposed. He and LaFarge, however, did not carry their preference for old Samoan customs to the point of adopting the native want of costume. They feared ridicule, not to mention mosquitoes.

Everywhere they asked their hosts endless questions about customs, families, and religion, and everywhere they ran into the same stubborn secrecy. Adams became convinced that under the superficial layer of their converted Christianity the Samoans preserved a secret priesthood mightier than the political chiefs, with supernatural powers, invocations, prophecies, charms, and the whole paraphernalia of paganism. The natives never

29

had to kill a missionary. They merely played him off.

On their *malangas*, or boat excursions, to the smaller islands, the two friends thrust themselves deeper and deeper into the Polynesian mystery. How had the natives ever got there? From east or west? Was Darwin correct about the origin of coral reefs? LaFarge despaired of duplicating the quality of the light, and Adams of catching the true expression of the islands. To John Hay, Adams wrote that it was languor that was not languid, voluptuousness that was not voluptuous, a poem without poetry. At other moments it struck him as simply an im-

them. LaFarge, alone, might have.

Before leaving Samoa, they became fairly intimate with Robert Louis Stevenson, who had moved there with his wife and mother, in the last round of his gallant but desperate struggle with tuberculosis. Stevenson's letter to a friend in England about their first visit caused much hilarity when the Adams circle got hold of it: "Two Americans called on me yesterday. One, an artist named LaFarge, said he knew you. The name of the other I do not recall."

Stevenson was immediately congenial with LaFarge,

When LaFarge painted three Samoans carrying a canoe, he was reproached by the girl at left. She was "of high origin," LaFarge wrote later, and resented being shown working with lower-class friends. At right above, he paints Samoan girls making up kava, a peppery native drink. The painter found the drink itself "curious," but he was enchanted with the girls' sinuous movements as they prepared it.

possible stage decoration. Gazing at the natives passing his cottage in their blue or red or yellow waistcloths, their bronzed skins aglow in the sun against the surf line of the coral reef, he wrote Anna Lodge that he expected to see a prima donna in green garlands and a girdle of ti leaves emerge from the next hut to invoke the cuttlefish or the shark with a Wagnerian chorus of native maidens.

But in the end reality surpassed all such images. Perhaps Adams' most vivid memory would be the picnic by the sliding rock where they watched the yellow limbs of the girls who plunged naked into the white foam, like goldfish in a blue-green pool. LaFarge said that had they stayed much longer they would have plunged in after

but he put Adams in mind of a dirty cotton bag over a skeleton. The novelist's flashing dark eyes, his darting body, his improbable tales, made Adams uneasy. Adams recoiled from physical messiness and may have ascribed what he saw of this quality to Stevenson's mental processes. In this he was certainly unfair. Adams had turned away from life in wandering to the Polynesian islands; Stevenson was searching for it. He gave all of himself to the Samoan experience; he dug roots, cut trees, and helped with the building of his house at Vailima like a man on the frontier. He entered passionately into the political disputes of the island and fiercely embraced the side of the natives against that of the exploiting colonials. Adams felt that Stevenson could never understand the Samoans because he attributed to them the motivations of boys in the Edinburgh of his own youth. But I wonder if Stevenson's understanding of boys and of adventure did not put him closer to the Samoans than Adams could ever have been.

After Samoa came the appalling disillusionment of Tahiti. Adams described it as an exquisitely successful cemetery. The atmosphere was one of hopelessness and premature decay. The natives were not the gay, big, animal creatures of Samoa; they were still, silent, sad in expression, and fearfully few in number. The population

bers of the deposed royal family, the Tevas. Next to Mataafa in Samoa, he found the old ex-queen of Tahiti, Hinari, or Grandmother, the most interesting native figure in the Pacific. She showed none of the secrecy of the Samoan chiefs but took a motherly interest in Adams and LaFarge and told them freely, sitting on the floor, all her clan's oldest legends and traditions. Adams was even adopted into the Teva clan and given the hereditary family name of Taura-atua, with the lands, rights, and privileges attached to it—though these holdings consisted of only a hundred square feet.

Without explanation of her unusual technique, John LaFarge labelled the picture of the Samoan girl above, Young Girl Weeding. *John's daughter-in-law, Mrs. Bancel LaFarge, painted Henry Adams (who was her uncle) in his Washington home in 1894. Adams didn't like pictures of himself, and he tore up this water color. The patient artist pieced it back together again, but the cracks are still visible.*

had been decimated by bacteria brought in by Westerners. Rum was the only amusement which civilization and religion had left the people. The puppet king, Pomare, was to die of a rotten liver shortly after Adams and LaFarge left. Tahiti was a halfway house between Hawaii and Samoa. Adams complained that a "pervasive half-castitude" permeated everything, "a sickly whitey-brown, or dirty-white complexion" that suggested weakness and disease.

He was bored, he insisted, as he had never been bored in the worst wilds of Beacon Street or at the dreariest dinner tables of Belgravia. While waiting for a boat to take them elsewhere, anywhere, he amused himself by returning to his role of historian and interviewing mem-

But when he came, some years later, to put the history into a book which he had privately printed, it was little more than an interesting failure. Tahiti had no history, in the Western sense of the word, until the arrival of the white man. Of the thousands of years that had preceded Captain Cook, where generation had succeeded generation without distinguishable change, there was nothing left but genealogy and legend. The genealogy, which makes up a large part of Adams' book, is boring, and as for the legend, he admitted himself that it needed the lighter hand of Stevenson.

Yet *The Memoirs of Arii Taimai* nonetheless mark an important step in Adams' career. He had gone, by 1890, as far as he was going as a historian in the conventional

sense. His great work on Jefferson and Madison was history at its most intellectually pure. The author stands aside and lets the documents tell the story, from which a very few precious rules may be deduced. But in the South Seas he had tried to leave the intellect for simplicity, for instinct. He had sought peace and found ennui. Even the unspoiled natives, in the long run, palled. He had to return, in Papeete, to his profession, and he had to try it with a new twist, for how else could Tahitian history be done? And if *The Memoirs* were a bore, was it altogether his fault? Might it not be in the subject? Suppose he were to happen upon a subject that required not only the imagination of the man who had sat on the floor with the old queen of Tahiti as she intoned the poems of her family tradition, but also the industry of the devoted scholar who had pored through archives of European foreign offices? Suppose he were to find a subject, in short, that required a great artist as well as a great historian?

He was to find such a one a few years hence in the Gothic cathedrals of France. *Mont-Saint-Michel and Chartres* is an extraordinary tour de force of the imagination, a vivid invocation of the spirit and force of the twelfth century that may be longer read than any of Adams' other books. It has always been a difficult volume for librarians to classify. Is it history or travel or criticism or theology or even fiction? But its language shimmers with some of the magic blue of the windows of the cathedral which forms its principal topic. One day, at the Metropolitan Museum of Art, gazing at the brilliant *Ia Orana Maria*, I was struck by the fact that the Virgin of Chartres, like the Virgin of Paul Gauguin, may owe something to the colors and legends of the South Seas.

Gauguin arrived in Tahiti a few days after Adams and LaFarge had left, in time to witness the funeral of King Pomare. It is probably just as well that they did not meet. The American travellers detested European settlers, and a European settler who drank to excess and lived publicly with a native woman would have seemed the acme of Western corruption. If Adams had considered Stevenson a Bohemian, Gauguin would have been beyond the pale. Nor would LaFarge have liked Gauguin's painting. Many years later, when he and Adams were old men and Gauguin was dead, LaFarge wrote to his former travelling companion about an illustrated catalogue of a Gauguin show in Paris. He informed Adams that the "mad Frenchman" had been in Tahiti shortly after their visit and had actually met some of their friends on the island. It is disappointing to have to relate that LaFarge then went on to say that Gauguin's paintings were sorry failures, desperate efforts to

The solitary fisherman opposite, waiting with his spear poised in the calm waters of a Samoan lagoon, was painted by John LaFarge in 1890. At right is the Stevenson menage in front of the writer's house in Samoa at about the time Adams and LaFarge visited there. Seated in chairs in the center of the photograph are Robert Louis Stevenson and his wife. Stevenson's mother sits facing them at their right, and in combinations of native and European clothing, members of the household staff cluster around their employer.

catch the attention of a novelty-hunting public.

It has been said that Gauguin, with his brilliant colors and primitive figures, caught the essential atmosphere of the islands that both Adams and LaFarge missed. But what he really did was to create a Polynesia of his own that millions of his admirers now regard as the true one. Gauguin came to Tahiti naïvely in search of an island paradise, an unspoiled Arcadia, but he found and recognized in Papeete precisely what Adams had found and recognized. Only on canvas could he realize his dream. He was under no illusions about what he was doing. His red seas and blue dogs were perfectly deliberate. He wanted painting to stand independent of what it purported to represent and not to be a branch of sculpture. He said that the kind of people who wanted exact reproduction would have to wait for the invention of a color camera. They have, and they are quite content!

Of the brilliant four who were in the Polynesian islands in 1891—Adams, Stevenson, Gauguin, and LaFarge—the first three, like most artists, brought more with them than what they were to take out. The subjective experiences of the historian, of the storyteller, and of the postimpressionist might have been very much the same in other parts of the globe. Polynesia simply happened to be the stage of one aspect of their development. But in LaFarge's work I feel a more objective effort to re-

produce the islands than the others may have made.

His stubborn imagination fixed them in a classic atmosphere that seemed proof against disillusionment. To him the blues and greens were painted in lines of Homer, guessed at by Titian, and the long sway and cadence of the surf had the music of the Odyssey. The Samoan youngster with a red hibiscus fastened in his hair by a grassy knot was a Bacchus of Tintoretto. LaFarge prided himself on having an affinity with a remoter ancestry of man and on being better able than other Westerners to understand the islanders.

But if his paintings have a charm that may be special and Polynesian, they are nevertheless romantic. They tell us quite as much of John LaFarge as they do of the South Seas. Perhaps it is because he insisted that the paradise still existed which Gauguin knew was dead. And perhaps this very insistence is the one good thing that came out of the meeting of East and West. The dream of innocence, abided in or awoken from, may still be a mighty source of inspiration.

Mr. Auchincloss is both a novelist and a practicing lawyer as well as president of the Museum of the City of New York. His newest book, called Second Chance, Tales of Two Generations, *will be issued in the autumn by the Houghton Mifflin Company of Boston.*

The New Nostalgia... Many Happy Returns

By BARBARA KLAW

CHARLES E. TUTTLE & CO., INC.

An anthropologist studying the reading habits of Americans at the turn of the late, unlamented decade would find some revealing contrasts. On the one hand he would note the smashing success of *Portnoy's Complaint*—with more than 600,000 hardcover copies sold as of the end of 1969—and dozens of other fast-selling titillations. On the other, quite opposite, hand he would find that Americans by the hundreds of thousands were also reading nostalgia—volume after volume of unabashed, hard-core nostalgia.

Of course books that appeal to our affectionate memories have always been around, but the rush of them, and the numbers sold, have been quite phenomenal in the last year or two.

The current epidemic probably started with the publication in 1968 of a facsimile edition of the 1897 Sears Roebuck catalogue, a venture that a smart young publishing firm, Chelsea House, launched in a modest fashion. The idea was suggested by their advisory editor, Fred L. Israel, who also teaches history at City College in New York. Israel decided to assign the Sears Roebuck catalogue to his students to illustrate points in his lectures about American living styles at the end of the nineteenth century. Finding the catalogues very hard to come by, he guessed that a larger audience than his students might respond to the delights of the one elusive early catalogue he managed to locate. Chelsea House, a small company that distributes its books through larger publishers, took the idea around to six firms—all of which yawned politely—before finding one, Random House, that agreed to distribute the book.

Chelsea House printed only five thousand copies at first. "We didn't even put a dust jacket on it," Harold Steinberg, the president of Chelsea House, said. "We thought its sale would be entirely to libraries." At last count the sale of the book, at $14.95, has exceeded 140,-000 copies, and it is still selling briskly—to its publisher's unutterable delight. Other publishers have hurried into print with the 1902, 1903, 1908, and 1927 Sears catalogues; the 1902 number has sold over 400,000 copies in hard-cover and paperback form for $6.95 and $3.95, respectively. Perhaps the finest feat of salesmanship in the whole venture was selling the book back to Sears Roebuck itself. The mail-order store bought ten thousand copies from Chelsea House as gifts and has also been selling the facsimile of its 1897 catalogue ($14.47) through its new catalogue (free to loyal customers).

The publishing formula for nourishing our appetite for nostalgia varies, but one of the most successful—witness the 1897 Sears catalogue—is to find an old yet familiar item, print a facsimile of it, embellish it with new front matter, package it handsomely, and sell it for a large sum. This procedure has certain obvious advantages for the publisher. The volume chosen is often old enough for any copyright to have expired, editorial costs are negligible, and the illustrations are built in.

In selling books for the nostalgia market, Steinberg said that Chelsea House is searching for "things that strike us as having a resonance. We publish these books exactly as they originally appeared, just giving them a new frame. So you could say that we are selling very inexpensive antiques or artifacts."

The 1897 Sears Roebuck catalogue, or *Consumers Guide* as it was then called, is an "artifact" to make the reader's mouth water. As S. J. Perelman says in an introduction to the volume called "Browsers' Delight," the cover of the catalogue sports "a rather overweight divinity—Ceres, the corn and earth goddess, I judged—posed beside a cornucopia from which gush forth a variety of goodies— upright pianos, wardrobes, stoves, et cetera." Over six thousand items are listed in the index, Perelman points out, ranging "from autoharps to kraut cutters, from dulcimers to teething rings, from foot scrapers to feather boas." Or, to be strictly alphabetical, from abdominal corsets to zulu guns.

The copy accompanying this profusion of goods is what we would now call the hard sell. Richard Sears, who is reputed to have written personally every one of the millions of words of text in these 786 pages (except, possibly, the testimonials from satisfied customers), doesn't just describe: he exhorts, cajoles, and plots with the customers to run their local retail stores out of business. "Our factory to consumer system may be hard on the middleman, but it's easy on the consumer. Which class deserves the most consideration?" a marginal note asks. Sears also sprinkles the text with epigrams and puns. For example, on a page describing men's furnishings is the stern admonition "Shiftless He Who Shirtless Goes." And under ladies' summer union suits, he writes, "In union there is strength."

For the modern browser, however, the most startling thing about the *Consumers Guide* is the prices. If the portable forge for $6.30, or the popcorn popper for eight cents, or the seven-foot miner's tent, complete with poles, for $2.30 doesn't get to us, surely the man's cashmere overcoat for $5.25, twelve-pound pails of imported herring for eighty-five cents, or a four-panel wooden door (weight twenty-two pounds) for $1.10 will set up wistful vibrations.

Among the other memory feasts that have been offered to the public in facsimile recently is a Montgomery Ward catalogue that is even older than the Sears *Consumers Guide*; it dates from the year 1895. Jumping quickly ahead, there is also the 1922 Montgomery Ward version. (By then, apparently, do-it-yourself mining, at least at Montgomery Ward, was out, for the prospector's tent isn't even listed.) Another particularly charming entry is *The American Girls Handy Book*, reissued by its original publisher

in 1969. This practical guide to "How to amuse yourself and others" was originally written in 1887 by Adelia B. and Lina Beard. The Beard sisters designed their book as a companion piece to *The American Boys Handy Book*, written five years earlier by their brother Daniel C. Beard, who later founded the Boy Scouts of America. This one was also reissued in 1969. The reader detects a certain feminist streak in the Beard girls; they state in their preface that the book is for "the American boy's neglected sisters." Nor did they go along with the concept that nice little girls of the 1880's should confine themselves to painting china or embroidering (although these subjects are covered, too). For instance, they urge girls to take up tennis, and they start the section with exact specifications for making one's own tennis net.

The most recent facsimile reprint is the 1929 Johnson Smith catalogue, published in April of this year. For $10.00 we can recall the jokes and tricks that wowed us when we were children. Items like "the whoopee cushion" or "the joy buzzer" ("under the sheet it feels like a mouse") entranced a whole generation of little boys, and in the heyday of the company thousands of them mailed off their dimes and nickels to get such thigh-slappers as the melting spoon or the black-eye joke ("It isn't a bad joke if your friend isn't hot tempered"). The Johnson Smith Company also sold—and still sells on a much smaller scale—office equipment, musical instruments, books, and jewelry; but what most of us remember, the items with the "resonance," are the practical jokes—objects that parents of the day tended to regard as junk. Although it is still too early to know how this one will sell, a sampling of the Johnson Smith catalogue was printed as a dollar pamphlet in December of 1969, and thirty

CHELSEA HOUSE

Buck Rogers became more muscular and Wilma more voluptuous during the comic strip's long life, but their characters remained wholesome.

OUR $34.00 MICHIGAN A GRADE COMBINATION
Market and Pleasure Wagon.

This Is a Strictly A Grade Wagon,

GUARANTEED BY A BINDING
GUARANTEE FOR TWO YEARS.

OUR SPECIAL PRICE IS

$34.00
On Regular C. O.
D. Terms.

THREE PER CENT DISCOUNT

Allowed if cash in full accompanies your order, in which case $33.00 pays for the rig.

THIS WAGON IS MADE IN JACKSON, MICH.

By One of the Largest and Most Reliable
Wagon Manufacturers in America.

DESCRIPTION.

BODY. Body is made from the very best selected material, heavily ironed throughout with Norway iron; is 7 feet long, 24 inches wide and 8 inches deep. Comes with a foot board, one seat, long 34 inch riser, and flare boards. GEAR. Gear is from the best selected second growth hickory: combination single perch; elliptic springs in rear of same; elliptic springs in front; 1¼ inch axle. WHEELS. Sarven's patent, 14 Inch tread; ½ inch tire, full bolted. Wheels are guaranteed in every respect. PAINTING. It is painted in a thoroughly first class manner, body dark green, handsomely striped; gear dark green or red with suitable striping TRIMMINGS. Imitation leather or corduroy, as desired.

No. 95143.

WEIGHT OF WAGON, 500 POUNDS. CRATED IT WEIGHS ABOUT 550 POUNDS. CAPACITY, 1000 POUNDS.

At the Special Prices Named of $34.00 on Regular Terms or $33.00 Cash with Order we Furnish the
Wagon Complete with Shafts.

THE PRICE QUOTED IS FOR THE WAGON CRATED and delivered on board the cars at Jackson, Michigan, from which point you must pay the freight. By referring to the freight rates in front of book you will see that the freight will amount to next to nothing as compared with what you save in price.

Extra for pole with neckyoke and whiffletrees complete in place of shafts, $2.00. Width of track, either 4 feet 8 inches or 5 feet 2 inches, as desired. In ordering, be sure to state width of track wanted.

GLAD SUNSHINE RANGE.
For hard or soft coal, with Reservoir.

No. 15836.

No. 15836. Though low in price, quality has not been sacrificed to price in the construction of this range. It has all the latest improvements—ventilated oven, solid end hearth, duplex grate, patent pedal attachment, quick draft damper, etc. We are inclined to think that nothing so good and serviceable has ever before been offered for the money required to buy this range. This range has six holes.

Size.	Size of Covers.	Size of Oven.	Shipping Weight.	Price.
80	8 in.	17x18x11½	306 lbs.	$19.00
18	8 in.	19x20x12	345 lbs.	21.60

WATCH FOR $7.95

No. 65085.

For Engraving on watch cases: Script, 2½ cents per letter; Old English, 5½ cents.

Infants' French Kid Button.

No. 3765 This Shoe is made from a choice selection of genuine kid fancy stitched, has kid sole, and is a very pretty shoe for an infant. Cut very full so you will have no trouble to put them on. Color, tan. Sizes, 1, 2, 3 and 4.
Per pair..........$0.40
No. 3766 The same style, in dongola kid. Black only. Sizes, 1, 2, 3 and 4.
Per pair..........$0.25

No. 23660. Bust Pads, the kind that usually sold for 50 cents. Our price.............................25¢

LADIES' SUMMER UNION SUITS.
IN UNION THERE IS STRENGTH.

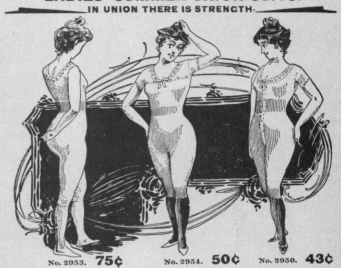

No. 2953. **75¢** No. 2954. **50¢** No. 2950. **43¢**

CHALLENGE PRICES IN MENS
BLACK AND BLUE CHEVIOTS SUITS.

Nº1 Nº2 Nº4 Nº3

$5·75 $6·50 $7·00 $7·50 $8·00 $9·00 $10·00

PRICES GUARANTEED BELOW ALL OTHERS.

Full Beards.

25838 On wire... $0.80
25839 Ventilated..1.75

25840 Mustashe on wire spring, common.
Each.........$0.10
Per dozen.........75

$1.95 Buys a $3.25 Hat.

The Evette.

23465 A Regular $3.25 Trimmed Hat for $1.95. Economical Lovers of Stylish Hats Save just $1.30 when they buy this hat.
This hat is made of a fancy rough straw and is trimmed with a ruffle of ribbon and lace around crown and band of jet, loop of lace and plume on side, finished with large rosette of lace, turned up in back and finished with rosette of ribbon. People wanting a fine hat cheap, should order this hat; it is a bargain rarely seen. Each... $1.95

Our $3.00 Puff Bang.

25820 Puff Bang. Parted in the latest style. made for fine trade. on ventilated foundation, with hair lace part.
See cut.
Each............$3.00

thousand copies were appreciatively snapped up by the end of the month, presumably to stuff adult Christmas stockings.

As well as digging out items to print in facsimile, publishers have been thinking up tempting anthologies for the nostalgia market. In late 1969, for instance, Christmas shoppers could choose between *The Saturday Evening Post Treasury*, in which the list of contributors reads like a course in American fiction (plus thirty-two pages of "classic cover paintings"), or the more frankly camp volume, *Parlour Poetry*, designed to reintroduce the "recital poetry" that "thrived in Victorian parlours." This collection includes such rousers as "Barbara Frietchie" and "The Charge of the Light Brigade" as well as lachrymose staples such as "My Mother's Bible" and "The Lips that Touch Liquor Shall Never Touch Mine."

The Collected Works of Buck Rogers in the 25th Century, which sold twenty-five thousand copies in its first month in the bookstores, is perhaps the largest and glossiest of these anthologies, produced with the respect that might characterize a book about cathedrals. For $12.50 the reader can race through twelve whole episodes of the now defunct comic strip without waiting, as contemporary enthusiasts were forced to do, for the next edition of their newspaper to reveal how Buck and his girl friend Wilma managed to escape once again from the menacing clutches of the Red Mongols. Buck and Wilma remain perennially young, in comic-strip fashion, but they

reflect the passing years: Buck grows more muscular and Wilma distinctly bustier. If their rocket ships and atomic guns no longer seem so fanciful today, there is still mystery in "inertron," the miraculous element that falls away from the earth, and an appealing innocence about such expletives as "Satan's Beard!"

The most unusual of the current deluge of reprints is a book that only a few thousand people ever saw when it was originally written in 1886. Called *Professional Criminals of America*, it was written by Inspector Thomas Byrnes, who was then chief of the New York City Detective Bureau. Byrnes's book (which its current publishers refer to among themselves as "the crook book") contains pictures and biographical sketches of 204 of the leading

criminals of the day. It was an era when crime in the United States was becoming a social institution, "a parody, as reflected in a crazy mirror, of the existing business system," as Professor Arthur M. Schlesinger, Jr., says in his introduction to the reissue. Byrnes comments on the phenomenon himself. "Robbery is now classed as a profession," he says, "and in the place of the awkward and hang-dog-looking thief we have today the intelligent and thoughtful rogue."

Byrnes was a highly successful cop, although some of his methods were somewhat less than ethical. He made deals with criminals that permitted them to pursue their careers unmolested in San Francisco, Minneapolis, or Chicago, for instance, as long as they kept out of New York. Or even more specifically, he often allowed them to operate in the poorer sections of the city if they kept

The black-eye joke, above left, produces only a synthetic black eye, while Ventrilo, used as suggested above, may well produce a real one. In addition to its mouse-under-the-sheet effect, left, the joy buzzer is guaranteed effective on the seats of chairs.

their agile fingers out of the pockets of its wealthy citizens. He even went so far as to lay down a "Dead Line" around the financial district; any suspicious character found on the affluent side of that boundary would be picked up on sight. Criminals, it was said, knew the rules so well that they took the precaution of getting a pass from one of Byrnes's men when they had legitimate business to transact downtown.

Byrnes's book, which one modern reviewer has described as "a coffee table book that won't just lie there," was written with the idea of thwarting criminals by making their faces familiar to the public. Now, in 1970, it seems a benign and nostalgic volume. There is a minimum of violence to jar the reader, since Byrnes's

Needless to say, the page at left is our composite, not an actual page, from Sears's 1897 Consumers Guide. *The prices are astonishing.*

professionals were mostly out for money rather than blood. Even the terminology of crime in the 1880's sounds less threatening than today's version. The criminals of 1886 fall into such categories as sneaks, stalls, swindlers, hotel men, dishonest servants, bunco steerers, toolmakers, and satchel workers. And Byrnes includes such fascinating specialists as Funeral Wells, a pickpocket who plied his trade only at funerals; James Titterington (alias Titter), a butcher-cart thief; Mollie Matches, a robber who disguised himself as a match girl; and Hugh L. Courtenay, a bogus English lord who swindled susceptible ladies, using such diverse and colorful aliases as Lord Courtney, Lord Beresford, or Sir Harry Vane of Her Majesty's Lights. ("The party's right name is supposed to be Clinton," Byrnes remarks, "and he is the son of a former lodge-keeper of the Earl of Devon.")

For the cleverer thieves, Byrnes's admiration almost gets out of hand. One bank robber named Rufus Minor, for instance, he describes as "no doubt one of the smartest bank sneaks in America. . . . He is a very gentlemanly and intelligent man . . . and it is a pity he is a thief." This is particularly high praise, since Byrnes has earlier stated that bank thieves in general are top of the heap—"men of education, pleasing address, good personal appearance and faultless in their attire." Less exalted specialists could also win his praise, though. There is Poodle Murphy, a pickpocket who "is without doubt the smartest pickpocket in America. He is the man who does the work, while his confederates annoy the victim and attract his attention." Although Byrnes in general is more restrained about female operatives, occasionally they, too, earn his respect. "Little Annie Reilly," he writes, "is considered the cleverest woman in her line in America. She generally engages herself as a child's nurse, makes a great fuss over the children, and gains the good will of the lady of the house. She seldom remains in one place more than one or two days before she robs it." Six weeks after publication in 1969 Byrnes and his compendium of crooks had made their way onto, or off of, twenty thousand coffee tables.

It is impossible to guess how long the current vogue for nostalgia will continue, but it is fun to speculate about what will set off the resonance fifty years from now. If this season's successes are any indication, it will obviously be some item that recalls to Americans of the 2020's a simpler, cheaper, less threatening, funnier, or more personal time. Will it be a facsimile of a 1970's clothing catalogue, recalling that quaint time when people still put all those garments on their bodies? Will it be a visual anthology of television commercials from the mid-twentieth century? Perhaps luscious pictures of vegetables and meats will be what stirs that future generation, presumably nourished entirely on pills and seaweed. Or will it simply be a book?

Annie Reilly, dishonest servant, is well worth knowing. Has stolen more in the last fifteen years than any other four women.

James Wells, alias "Funeral Wells," pickpocket. His line is picking pockets at funerals. Known in all principal cities.

Terrance Murphy, alias Poodle Murphy, alias Robinson, pickpocket. Poodle's picture is excellent, if somewhat drawn.

A GALLERY OF ROGUES, 1886,

as photographed and described (in somewhat abbreviated form) by Inspector Byrnes

James Titterington, butcher-cart thief. He branched out as a sneak thief, burglar, then a highwayman.

Rufus Minor, alias Rufe Pine, bank sneak. Can quickly grow heavy beard. Removes it after committing crime.

Hugh L. Courtenay, a bogus lord, swindler. A slim build. Claims to be married, which is not a fact.

JOHN LARNEY
alias Mollie Matches; Pickpocket, Bank Burglar, etc.

Record: Although a talented thief, Mollie was always an out-spoken one, to which failing he ultimately owed his downfall. During the war Mollie attained great eminence as a bounty jumper. He says he enlisted in ninety-three regiments. At a Massachusetts state prison from which he escaped, he had the freedom of the jail yard on account of his eyesight fail-ing him; he recovered his eyesight and liberty both. The adventures through which this man passed are wonderful.

MARY ANN CONNELLY
alias Elizabeth Irving, alias Haley, alias Taylor; Pickpocket, Shoplifter and Bludgeon Worker

Description: Fifty years old in 1886. Born in Ireland. Very fleshy, coarse woman. Height, about 5 feet 4 inches. Weight, 240 pounds. Black hair, black eyes, ruddy complexion. Talks with somewhat of an Irish brogue. Record: She is a well known New York pickpocket, shoplifter and prostitute, and a coarse, vulgar woman, that would stop at nothing to carry her point. Her picture is an excellent one, taken in 1875.

INFLAMMATORY ART

In one of the Beatles' famous songs, "Penny Lane," there is a fireman who keeps his fire engine clean (it's a clean machine, very clean). But that's about all that can be done to spruce up an apparatus nowadays, when the machines, like almost everything else, are produced by assembly lines, and fire-engine red is the only color tolerated. During the first half of the nineteenth century, when most American fires were put out, or not put out, by volunteer fire companies, the hand-operated pumpers were lavishly trimmed and decorated in a broad spectrum of vivid hues. The dazzling decor of a company's machine was as much a matter of jealous pride as how far the thing could be made to squirt.

This was partly because in every American community volunteer fire companies were a lively and important part of the social and political scene. In cities like New York, Chicago, or Baltimore they played much the same role that fraternities do on college campuses. You had to be invited to join; there was a prestige hierarchy depending on the social and business background of the members of a particular company; and once you were "in," you loyally maintained that yours was by all odds the best outfit in the city. Its superiority had to be demonstrated whenever possible—by getting to a fire faster than any other company in your part of town, pumping water higher and quicker, rescuing more pretty ladies in daring feats of ladder acrobatics, and if necessary administering fistic correction to any company that too aggressively disputed the field. (Quite a few houses burned to the ground while rival companies engaged in all-out brawls at the scene of the conflagration.) You also had to have equipment that was stunningly attractive, both rich and gaudy in appearance.

The design of the old hand-pump engines offered obvious places for decorative panels—especially the housing of the pump itself—and local artists were called upon to paint appropriate pictures. The Tammany tiger, for instance, was once an emblem on the pumper of a New York company whose foreman was William M. "Boss" Tweed. Thomas Sully, the well-known artist, executed a portrait of Lafayette for the Lafayette Hose Company of Philadelphia in 1833. More often the painter was an amateur, and the motif more general, with a preponderance on the side of allegorical patriotism. Among other things this gave a chance for art that ordinarily would have been considered daring, since everyone knew that goddesses of liberty, equality, and other democratic abstractions had a natural penchant for careless décolletage.

The stirring examples of nineteenth-century fire-engine panels displayed on the following pages are all from the collection of the Peale Museum, in Baltimore, and each was once the pride and delight of a volunteer company in that city. We present them here with thanks to the museum's director, Mr. Wilbur H. Hunter, who had them cleaned and photographed, and who has supplied us with pertinent information.—*The Editors*

The fire engine under the title is a detail from a certificate of membership issued by a Baltimore company in 1850. Opposite: perhaps a bit plump by Playboy *standards, this insouciant nymph was a sensation at Baltimore fires over a century ago.*

40

Many of the fire-engine painters were distinctly on the primitive side, and their allegories sometimes were obscure. It is not clear why the goddess of liberty opposite is letting the American eagle weep into her chalice—or is it that his beak is watering? The one above is much more explicit: she tramples monarchy while pointing out a thing or two in the great Declaration.

The world of Wagnerian opera seems to have over-taken this pair of panels. Although he is spurning the crown, scepter, and shackles of tyranny, the hero above doesn't give the impression of being entirely anti-authoritarian himself. His mate, opposite, makes Brünnhilde look like a piker: she has a crew of lusty tars, an eagle who eats the links of serfdom like pretzels, and Triton with his seahorses and skindivers.

A RIDE FOR LIFE
IN A BUFFALO HERD

By OTHNIEL C. MARSH

With an introduction by James Penick, Jr.

Othniel Charles Marsh lived a strenuous life full of achievement. He helped found the Peabody Museum of Natural History and the United States Geological Survey. He exposed the Indian Ring in the Grant administration and forced the resignation of a Cabinet officer, Secretary of the Interior Columbus Delano. He served as president of the National Academy of Sciences for three consecutive terms. His friends included Charles Darwin, Thomas Huxley, and the Sioux Nation. His enemies—notably his bitter scientific rival, an unpacific Quaker named Edward Drinker Cope—were at least as interesting. Marsh spent his entire personal fortune to maintain an army of bone diggers in the field, who eventually shipped to the Peabody, from all over the West, a staggering life-time haul of thirty freight-car loads of fossils that helped establish Marsh's reputation as a vertebrate paleontologist.

Yet in his autobiography, of which he completed only five fragmentary chapters before his death in 1899, his thoughts turned away from impressive deeds and back to the time when as a young assistant professor he had led parties of Yale seniors over the high plains and central Rockies, braving bad water, voracious insects, and hostile Indians, in search of fossils. What the aging Marsh savored in his memory was the still-vivid thrill of hobnobbing with hard-bitten cavalrymen and notorious characters like Buffalo Bill, and of riding for his life in the middle of a stampeding herd of buffalo, the wind in his face and a canny Indian pony beneath him.

—J. P., Jr.

In October, 1872, I was exploring the chalk cliffs of western Kansas for fossils . . . The region under exploration, along the Smoky Hill River and its tributaries, between Fort Hays and Fort Wallace, was then [the Cheyennes'] special hunting ground, as the buffalo were there in countless numbers, and herds of thousands were daily in sight from the bluffs on which we were at work.

Our party was a small one, a few Yale students, and a small military escort from Fort Wallace, consisting of Lieutenant Pope, a sergeant, and about a score of soldiers. This escort I owed to General Sherman [the famous Civil War commander who was the Army's General in Chief, 1869–84], a faithful friend in all my western explorations. I appreciated his kindness all the more, as just then the frontier posts had none too many troops to keep the Indians in check. Our guide was the famous Ned Lane, known over that whole region for his knowledge of the country, especially of the Indians then infesting it. . . .

One afternoon, when returning from a long fossil hunt, the guide, Lieutenant Pope, and myself were riding slowly abreast, discussing the day's fossil hunt and the prospect for the morrow, from which I expected important results. . . . As we rode to the crest of a high ridge, the guide now slightly ahead, as is usual in an Indian country, suddenly called out, "Great God, look at the buffalo!" and we saw a sight that I shall never forget, and one that no mortal eye will ever see again. The broad valley before us, perhaps six or eight miles wide, was black with buffalo, the herd extending a dozen miles, up and down the valley, and quietly grazing, showing that no Indians were near. The animals were headed to the South, and slowly moving up the valley in the direction . . . where pasturage for the night was to be found. The sight was so wonderful that we sat on our horses for some time, watching the countless throng, and endeavoring to make some estimate of how many buffalo were in sight before us. The lowest estimate was that of the guide, who placed the number at 50,000. I thought there were more; and our military comrade, with his mathematics fresh from West Point, made a rapid calculation of the square miles covered, and the number of animals to the mile, making his total nearly one hundred thousand. While we were thus engaged, the slowly declining sun behind us shed a golden light over the valley,

Something of the inexorable force that so terrified Othniel Marsh can be sensed in W. J. Hayes's painting Buffalo Herd on the Move.

the black moving masses being in strong relief, while our own lengthening shadows pointed toward the herd, that thus far had not deigned to notice us, all forming together a panorama of surpassing interest.

While wrapped in the wonderful prospect before us, the guide quietly remarked, "We must have one of those fellows for supper." This broke the spell and brought a practical question directly before us. The guide was mounted on a large mule, January by name, which had a long army record for nearly everything except buffalo hunting. Lieutenant Pope was on a tall cavalry horse, a new recruit that was gazing timidly on a herd of buffalo for the first time. My steed was a fleet Indian pony known as Pawnee, said to have been stolen from that tribe by a Sioux warrior, and well trained for the hunt by his former owners. He had proved his mettle in the two expeditions I had ridden him and in several chases I had given the buffalo then encountered. It was therefore at once decided that I must provide for our supper, and shifting my fossil treasures into the guide's saddle bags, and tightening the cinch of my pony and my own cartridge belt, I was soon ready for the fray. My hunting weapons consisted of a cavalry carbine and a pair of navy revolvers, not too many for an Indian country, and I hoped soon to bring down a young buffalo that would give our camp the wished-for meal. I rode slowly down toward the herd, avoiding a few old bulls outside the main body, so as not to disturb them. The wind was in my favor, and I soon was near the herd. Selecting my animal, I promptly gave chase, hoping to get in my shot before the herd started, which I knew would soon be the case. The animal selected, a young cow, proved especially fleet, and it was some minutes before I was alongside, ready to shoot, in the exact manner my first guide, Buffalo Bill, had taught me long before. While the chase was still going on, I had heard one or two shots behind me in the distance, and concluded that my comrades were firing at some straggling animal, but I had no time to look around, as my pony, knowing what was wanted, made a direct chase for the buffalo selected, and soon carried me where a shot from my carbine brought the animal to the ground. I then had a chance to look back.

To my amazement, I saw that the main herd, alarmed by the shots . . . had started and was moving rapidly southward. I saw also what I had not before surmised; that in my eagerness, I had pushed well into the herd without noticing it, and as the great mass of animals in the rear started, they began to lap around me, and I would soon be enclosed in the rapidly moving throng, liable at any moment to be trampled to death if my pony should fail me. My only chance of escape was evidently to keep moving with the buffalo and press towards the edge of the herd, and thinking thus to cut my way out, I began shooting at the animals nearest to me, to open the way. Each shot gave me some gain, as those near pushed away, and when one went down, others stumbled over him. The whole mighty herd was now at full speed, the earth seemed fairly to shake under the moving mass, which with tongues out, the flaming eyes and nostrils, were hurrying onward, pressed by those behind, up the broad valley, which narrowed as it approached the higher land in the distance. My horse was greatly excited by his surroundings, and at first seemed to think I wanted some particular animal, and was thus inclined to make chase after it, but he soon came to understand the serious problem before him, and acted accordingly.

A new danger suddenly confronted me. The prairie bottom had hitherto been so even that my only thought

CONTINUED ON PAGE 77

47

– George Eastman did

Descending Mount Vesuvius

The scene was London's Savoy Theatre on the evening of October 7, 1893, opening night of a new Gilbert and Sullivan operetta, *Utopia, Limited*. On stage Nekaya and Kalyba, "very modest and demure" twin girls, were singing a duet:

> *For English girls are good as gold,*
> *Extremely modest (so we're told) . . .*
> *To diagnose*
> *Our modest pose*
> *The Kodaks do their best:*
> *If evidence you would possess*
> *Of what is maiden bashfulness,*
> *You only need a button press—*
> *And we do all the rest.*

Like many of W. S. Gilbert's lyrics, this one reflected a very contemporary preoccupation—in this instance the Kodak craze, then rampant in Europe as well as America, the home of its originator, George Eastman. Born in upstate New York in 1854, Eastman at the age of twenty was a junior bookkeeper in a bank in Rochester. More significantly, he was a passionate amateur photographer and inventor who would become to the camera what Henry Ford would become to the automobile.

A shipboard scene

While photography had been practiced in this country since 1839, the bulkiness of the equipment and the complicated nature of the developing process strictly limited its appeal. As a young photographer, Eastman often carried up to seventy pounds of gear on his back; to take a picture he had to emulsify a fragile glass plate, expose it through the lens of his heavy camera, and—working fast before the emulsion dried—develop it under a hood. By 1885 he finally perfected a practicable gelatin-coated paper film that could be manufactured in rolls and packed inside a small camera. Within three years he had developed such a camera: small enough (3½ by 3¾ by 6½ inches) and light enough (twenty-two ounces) to be held in the hand. The operating instructions were extremely simple: 1. Point the camera; 2. Press the button; 3. Turn the key to position the next film frame; and 4. Pull the cord to recock the shutter. Not even a child could miss.

But Eastman knew it would take solid marketing and mass-production techniques to turn his ideas into gold. He named his camera Kodak—a short, catchy word that he coined himself and that was easy to pronounce in any language. He also developed the slogan paraphrased in Gilbert's lyric: "You press the button, we do the rest." Soon the Eastman Kodak Company was doing just that. For twenty-five dollars it was turning out a

"Ruth" at Thebes

camera complete with leather case and loaded with a one-hundred-exposure roll of film; after the pictures were taken the customer could ship case and camera, with the exposed film still inside, to Rochester, where for an additional ten dollars the factory would develop the film and send back a set of prints, along with the freshly reloaded camera. By 1889 there were thirteen thousand Kodak owners, and Eastman's staff was processing as many as 7,500 prints a day—all of them, until 1896, circular because of the shape of the image frame. By the turn of the century, when the Kodak Girl poster on page 48 appeared, a new folk art was thriving, and tens of thousands of Americans were heeding her advice and taking a Kodak with them wherever they went. Eastman set the example: he took the three photographs on page 49, probably on a trip abroad in 1889. And he was collecting many other photographs, amateur work that caught his eye.

The pictures on these two pages were among Eastman's own favorites, taken by customers long forgotten, and are now in the collection of the George Eastman House, Rochester. They were duplicated for the company's files from the hundreds of thousands of negatives sent in for developing. Little is known about the subjects or the photographers: though the company sold a little record book with its camera, few customers filled in the blanks faithfully. The scene at left center on the opposite page is labelled "Wagon train going west, Kingston, New York, 1888," and the young lady at top right on the same page is identified as "Marion Sawyer, Easthampton, Massachusetts, 1890." But no one knows where or when the train was wrecked or what beach the father and son below were exploring when a now-anonymous Kodak owner pressed the button and waited for Eastman to do the rest.
—*Carla Davidson*

FACES FROM THE PAST–XXIV

In January, 1917, outside a New York courtroom, the crowd behaved predictably: the same whispers and sly grins, the same ugly innuendoes and unreasoning anger, greeted her whenever she appeared in public; alone, facing them down, was the little woman with the shy smile and dark, penetrating eyes, quietly determined to speak her mind and persuade those who opposed her of the sanity of her cause. A few months earlier Margaret Sanger had opened the first American birth-control clinic; as a result she had been arrested several times, and now she was charged with violating a state law that prohibited distribution of literature on contraception. The judge promised leniency if she would agree to abide by the law in the future, but Margaret Sanger was determined to test the statute. "I cannot promise to obey a law I do not respect," she said, and was sentenced to thirty days in the workhouse, where she occupied her time by giving her fellow prisoners lectures on birth control.

The sixth of eleven children born to Michael Higgins, an Irish sculptor of tombstone angels in Corning, New York, Margaret had seen childbearing take her mother to an early grave; as a nurse she had come across babies "wrapped in newspapers to keep them from the cold; six-year-old children . . . pushed into gray and fetid cellars, crouching on stone floors, their small scrawny hands scuttling through rags, making lamp shades, artificial flowers." From the day in 1912 when Margaret Sanger decided to champion birth control, the enemy was never very far away. Arrayed against her were federal and state governments, churches, the medical profession, the press, and many of her friends, but if anyone personified the opposition, it was Anthony Comstock, a self-appointed "Guardian of Purity" who was incapable of distinguishing between information and obscenity. He had been largely responsible for persuading Congress to enact legislation in 1873 that barred "obscene, lewd, lascivious, filthy and indecent" materials from the U.S. mails. He had also succeeded in including contraceptive devices and literature about them under those headings, thus equating birth control with smut and pornography.

When in 1914 Margaret Sanger began publishing a paper, *The Woman Rebel*, that dealt with health, social hygiene, child labor, and the damaging effects of large families, the New York postmaster advised her that it could not be mailed. Not long afterward she was indicted by a grand jury on nine counts for alleged violations of federal statutes; if convicted, she could receive up to forty-five years in prison. When her case came up she asked for a stay, but the judge gave her only until the following morning. Even though it was wartime, she decided to flee to London, buying time to prepare her defense and publish a pamphlet she had just completed, called "Family Limitation," in which she presented the forbidden information about birth control. In 1916 she was back in the United States, brimming with practical information concerning new methods of contraception and with renewed determination to test America's antediluvian laws. When her trial began early in 1916, the government disappointed her by declining to prosecute (no test case meant that it was still against the law to advocate birth control).

The public, which heard so much about her views, knew very little of Margaret Sanger's private life. Her divorce from William Sanger, the father of her three children; her love affairs (including one with Havelock Ellis, the English authority on sex); her marriage in 1922 to J. Noah Slee, founder of the Three-in-One Oil Company, which brought her happiness and freedom from financial worry—none of these events overshadowed her determination to inform the public about birth control and to change the laws that prevented it. She hated speaking to large audiences, but she memorized a set talk that she delivered again and again. Her correspondence reached enormous proportions; she wrote constantly—books, tracts, articles; she founded clinics; she launched the American Birth Control League; she journeyed abroad to spread the word. And every step was dogged by controversy. By the time opposition from Protestant churches began to wane, the Catholic Church took up the fight with a vengeance. In 1921 an overflow crowd waiting outside New York's Town Hall for a birth-control rally was locked out on Archbishop Patrick Hayes's orders, and Margaret Sanger was arrested when she tried to speak. "Children troop down from Heaven because God wills it," the archbishop announced, and any attempt to prevent the increasing tide of humanity was "satanic." As late as 1929 her birth-control clinics in America were still being raided by police, prodded by the Catholic clergy.

Each flare-up of bigotry benefited her cause, bringing discussion of birth control out in the open, providing her with an opportunity to broadcast her views. Woman's fertility, she believed, was the chief cause of human misery and resulted in poverty, famine, and war. Fewer births would mean better and healthier children, more money for each member of a poor family, better-cared-for and better-educated young people. Until her eighty-sixth year Margaret Sanger persisted. She lived to see birth control acclaimed by most Protestant churches and by the American Medical Association; the courts liberalized the interpretation of existing laws. Birth-control instruction, which she had introduced, was available in hospitals and clinics; there was increased awareness of the tragedy implicit in unchecked population growth; birth control was saving the lives of many mothers, ending their ancient fear of constant pregnancy; and, partially through her efforts, people had begun to accept sex as a normal part of life. But after her death in 1966 the urgency remained: a recent Princeton University study indicates that of the population growth in the United States between 1960 and 1965, unwanted births accounted for 35 to 45 per cent.
—*Richard M. Ketchum*

Of Deathless Remarks...

By RICHARD HANSER

One day in 1921 a researcher rummaging through the archives of the *Service Hydrographique de la Marine* in Paris chanced upon a surprising document. What it was doing there and who wrote it have never been explained, but the paper turned out to be the only eyewitness account known to history of one of the high moments of the American Revolution. And it shockingly alters the picture America has always cherished of that great moment.

The document was a diary written in English by a Frenchman who had been visiting the American colonies. He may have been an agent of his government, but neither his name nor his mission is now known. The validity of the document itself, however, is not in doubt. It is full of detailed and intelligent comment on the geography, accommodations, customs, and people of the country its author passed through, and it is written objectively and without bias. The writer had no idea that he was damaging an American tradition at its birth.

On May 30, 1765, the diarist happened to be in Williamsburg, Virginia, when the House of Burgesses was in session. "I went immediately to the assembly," he wrote, "where I was entertained with very strong Debates Concerning Dutys that the parlement wants to lay on the American Colonys, which they Call or Stile stamp Dutys."

This, of course, was the day and the occasion when Patrick Henry, as tradition tells us, spoke the flaming words that every schoolboy knows, or should. "In a voice of thunder, and with the look of a god," his first and most famous biographer tells us, Patrick Henry rose in his seat and said: "Caesar had his Brutus—Charles the First, his Cromwell, and George the Third——"

Here came cries of "Treason! Treason!" from the assemblage. But, we are told, Henry "faltered not for an instant . . . [and] finished his sentence with the firmest emphasis—'*may profit by their example*. If *this* be treason, make the most of it.' "

It was a grand and unforgettable moment, a milestone on the glory road to rebellion, war, and independence.

Unfortunately, nobody took notes on the speech at the time—except our French traveller. And as the only eye- (or ear) witness on record, he gives us an ending different, and distinctly less thrilling, than the traditional one.

After the cries of "Treason!" according to our diarist, ". . . the Same member stood up again (his name is henery) and said that if he had afronted the speaker, or the house, he was ready to ask pardon, and he would shew his loyalty to his majesty King G. the third, at the Expence of the last Drop of his blood, but what he had said must be atributed to the Interest of his Countrys Dying liberty which he had at heart, and the heat of passion might have lead him to have said something more than he intended, but, again, if he said anything

The lithographers naturally concentrate on Patrick Henry's speech, not his apology.

wrong, he beged the speaker and the houses pardon . . ."

An apologetic Patrick Henry professing undying loyalty to the Crown and offering to bleed for his king is not quite what we're used to, but that is what the record—the only on-the-spot record—says. The speech as we know it and as it is given in the schoolbooks first appeared a half century after the event and is a work of historical paleontology by William Wirt, a Virginia lawyer and man of letters. Admitting that "not one of his [Henry's] speeches lives in print, writing, or memory," Wirt reconstructed the oration from the uncertain and fading recollections of a handful of aging men who were there, using a phrase from one and a sentence from another and fleshing out the body of the speech from his own imagination. What we have as one of the great American orations is actually a literary dinosaur pieced together out of a handful of memory bones and fossils.

Still, Patrick Henry did indeed say something inflammatory on that memorable day in the Virginia House of Burgesses. Though no account gives us his words verbatim, whatever he said caused something of a commotion. We know that the royal governor, Francis Fauquier, reported on the stamp debates to the Board of Trade in London and called attention to "very indecent language" used by "a Mr Henry a young lawyer." Weeks after the event, a London newspaper mentioned the speech with some indignation and reported that an unnamed member of the House had "blazed out" with references to Tarquin, Caesar, and Charles the First. (Tarquin disappears from the classic version of the speech, though the Frenchman's report includes him.) And Thomas Jefferson was present at the debate, standing in the lobby entrance of the hall, where he heard everything. When Wirt consulted him fifty years later, he "well remembered" Henry's fiery oratory and the defiant remarks about George the Third. If Henry backed down at the end, Jefferson didn't mention it to Wirt.

Nevertheless, it is impossible to get around those awkward notes of the itinerant Frenchman or to ignore the fact that William Wirt never heard or even saw Patrick Henry. Something of the same cloudiness surrounds the "liberty or death" speech, the very pinnacle of Revolutionary oratory, for which, again, we have only Wirt's undocumented version as a source.

On examination, a startling number of our most cherished sayings turn out to be of dubious provenance, the products of what the historian Daniel J. Boorstin has called "posthumous ghost-writing." He cites, among other instances, the celebrated slogan attributed to James Otis: "Taxation without representation is tyranny!" This has become an imperishable principle in the American credo and is endlessly quoted as the rallying cry of the Revolution. But it does not appear on the record anywhere until 1820, in the notes of John Adams.

Otis may have said it when he is credited with having said it, but we can't be sure now that he actually did. "From the era of the Revolution," Boorstin tells us, "the ringing words were those imagined to have been heard."

Did John Paul Jones, when called upon to strike his colors on the burning and battered *Bonhomme Richard*, reply: "I have not yet begun to fight"? He could have, but there is no proof that he did. He himself, in his own account of the battle, doesn't mention it, and it is unlikely that a man who got off a line like that would forget it. When the French demanded a bribe of $250,000 from the United States as the price of receiving the newly appointed American minister in 1797, did Charles Cotesworth Pinckney rise to the situation by thundering out the slogan "Millions for defense, but not one cent for tribute"? Well, no. What he said was: "No, no, not a sixpence!"—which, though just as emphatic, was not particularly memorable. The schoolbook-saying he is credited with was invented afterward by somebody else and transferred to Pinckney, who should have thought of it in the first place, but didn't.

Time and again, in all ages, the key figure in a dramatic event or historic situation has failed to produce the immortal words expected of him, or if he did there was nobody on hand to record them. The gap has often been filled by some volunteer ghost writer, contemporary or posthumous, who produced his version of what ought to have been said but unfortunately wasn't.

When, for instance, the Baron de Cambronne was called upon to surrender at the Battle of Waterloo, all France was thrilled at the report of his reply: *La Garde meurt, mais ne se rend pas*"—"The Guards die but do not surrender." To this day the words are inscribed on his statue in his home town of Nantes, and they have passed

L'Illustration

General Pershing comes silently ashore in France in 1917. It was someone else who said: "Lafayette, we are here!"

into other languages, including our own.

But the Baron himself repeatedly denied that he ever indulged in any such quote-book rhetoric, and the inescapable fact is that he did not die but was taken prisoner. What he actually said, he insisted, was *"Merde,"* which is still sometimes referred to in France as *le mot Cambronne.* A journalist who was nowhere near the battle invented the fancier version for him.

Voltaire would seem to be the last to need anyone's help in the creation of memorable phrases. Nevertheless, the one most often associated with him is not his. "I disapprove of what you say, but I will defend to the death your right to say it" cannot be found anywhere in his works. The words first appeared in 1906 in a book whose author considered them an accurate reflection of Voltaire's philosophy, and they seemed so right for him that they have been taken for granted as his ever since. In the same way Galileo's famous *"E pur si muove"*—"And yet it does move"—was put into his mouth long after his death. What he really said, if anything, after his recantation before the Inquisition on the movement of the earth around the sun is not known, but he could hardly have bettered *"E pur si muove,"* and it has become his just as irrevocably as if a shorthand stenographer had been present to take it down as it was uttered.

Despite the historian's obsession with accuracy and his passion for "as it actually happened" and all that, embellishment and invention often prove to be superior to literal truth when it comes to historic sayings and great phrases—the words men live by. In these matters the people themselves have long since decided that mere correctness is a trifle when weighed against the essential rightness, the poetry, the dramatic impact, of a given saying or familiar quotation.

So it makes little difference, from this viewpoint, whether William Tecumseh Sherman ever said "War is hell" in precisely those words. They are not discoverable in any of his writings or speeches. At a G.A.R. convention in Columbus, Ohio, on August 11, 1880, he said: "There is many a boy here today who looks on war as all glory, but, boys, it is all hell." The public, wielding its instinctive editorial pencil, shortened this to the more powerful and uncluttered three-word saying that is now standard and classic.

The public not only edits, shortens, and polishes, but it also invents, repeating words that were never uttered until they become imbedded in the national consciousness just as surely as if they had been truly spoken in the first place. Sherman, again, on his march to the sea was approaching the key supply depot at Allatoona, Georgia, when he learned that the place was under critical pressure by the enemy. Surveying the situation from Kennesaw Mountain, thirteen miles away, he sent off two messages to the Allatoona commander. One included the phrase "hold out" and the other "hold fast," and both included Sherman's promise he would soon arrive with relief. The two dispatches were subsequently condensed in the popular mind into "HOLD THE FORT! I AM COMING." Though the phrase was never actually used, "Hold the fort!" became a Union slogan and was put into a rousing revival hymn that swept the country.

No historic personage, no matter how eloquent or exalted, escapes this touching up, revision, and embellishment by the public, which seems to have a fairly infallible ear for the right sound and shape of a saying. When Winston Churchill took over as Prime Minister in Britain's most precarious hour of World War II, his first address to the House of Commons on May 13, 1940, included the sentence "I have nothing to offer but blood, toil, tears and sweat." The resonance and rhythm of the words was such that he subsequently used them over again, in the same order, on other crucial occasions during the war. They have been quoted thousands of times since—but seldom in the way Churchill first said them. The public ear apparently detected a hint of redundancy in "toil" and "sweat," and there was something in the word order that did not seem quite right. So, by the usual mysterious process of instinctive editing, the saying was revised to read "blood, sweat, and tears," which is how almost everyone now says it, including a rock group currently using the phrase as its billing. Anyone who quotes Churchill's original word order today sounds as if he has got it wrong.

It makes no difference at all how many times the correct form of a word or saying is brought before the public; if people decide they like another version better, that version will prevail. Tens of millions of draft notices, from World War I to Vietnam, have gone out with the plain, unmistakable salutation at the top: "Greeting." But in print and by word of mouth, the singular greeting from the government invariably comes out plural, as in the title of the recent movie about the draft, *Greetings.* But if *s* is added here where it doesn't belong, it sometimes arbitrarily disappears where it does belong. Franklin D. Roosevelt's group of academic and intellectual advisers was labelled a Brains Trust by James Kieran of the *New York Times,* but for some reason the plural offended the public ear and by tacit agreement was quickly dropped, though the British still keep it.

The public's insistence on having things said in its own way regardless of what actually was said has caused distress to more than one public figure. Herbert Hoover went to his grave insisting that he never called Prohibition "a noble experiment," and he didn't. What he called it was "a great social and economic experiment, noble in motive," which is not the same thing. But for as long as the subject is written about, "noble experiment" will be quoted derisively as a Hooverism, like "Prosperity

This English mezzotint of John Paul Jones in his battle with the Serapis *shows him "shooting a Sailor who had attempted to strike his Colours." Actually he hit the man with a pistol butt.*

Fathers" is one of the most durable, useful, and ubiquitous of all the phrases in the American lexicon. It is impossible to reach the age of twelve without coming across it or to write about the American past without using it. Yet it recently took a massive search by the Government and General Research Division of the Library of Congress to discover its author.

The search was instigated by the present writer, who needed the phrase for the script of a historical documentary. Twenty-three standard reference works were consulted without success. The best efforts of a professional researcher also proved fruitless. A number of authorities in the field confessed that they too were baffled. One of them had just completed a fat and exhaustive dictionary of American sayings but admitted he had no entry under "Founding Fathers"; rather than admit this inability to trace its origin he made no mention of the phrase at all.

Through the good offices of Representative Ogden Reid of New York, the Library of Congress was put to work on the matter. After several months of searching, which included combing through all the relevant historical literature from George Bancroft to the present, the originator of "Founding Fathers" was established as firmly as it is ever likely to be. His name could hardly have come as more of a surprise.

It was Warren Gamaliel Harding.

The first use of the phrase that the combined efforts of the experts at the Library of Congress have been able to find occurs in an address by Senator Harding before the Sons and Daughters of the American Revolution in Washington, on George Washington's birthday, 1918. "It is good," Senator Harding began, "to meet and drink at the fountains of wisdom inherited from the founding fathers of the republic."

He used it again in his speech on being officially notified of his nomination for the Presidency at Marion,

is just around the corner," which he didn't say either.

Worse, perhaps, than being saddled with something one did not say is to fade into history bereft of credit for a memorable mot one did in fact produce. "Founding

These pictures, taken at one time, show the lively platform manner of Warren G. Harding—mellifluous, active, ingratiating.

57

Ohio, on July 22, 1920, and yet again in his inaugural address on the Capitol steps on March 4, 1921. ("... I must utter my belief in the divine inspiration of the founding fathers.")

Since Harding now gets into the quotation dictionaries, if at all, chiefly on the strength of his neologism "normalcy" or in connection with the notorious "smoke-filled room," the revelation that "Founding Fathers" is his should raise him a considerable notch in future reference works. Not every President leaves an enduring phrase behind him. (Curiously, it was an Englishman who put the Library of Congress researchers on the right track. They found that Sir Denis Brogan, in his *Politics in America* (Harper, 1954), had correctly attributed the phrase to Harding. When I queried him as to how he had managed this feat when no one in America, apparently, could have done it, Sir Denis replied: "I arrived in the U.S.A. in September of 1925 when the memory of W. G. H. was fresh if not fragrant, and the information may have been common knowledge then. I may have picked it up by osmosis.")

Perhaps Harding's connection with his coinage was lost from sight because it seemed so unlikely. "Harding," said H. L. Mencken, "writes the worst English I have ever encountered; it reminds me of a string of wet sponges; it is so bad that a sort of grandeur creeps into it." His usual oratorical style is best described by a word he himself used—"bloviate"—which meant to make bloated speeches full of political clichés. Finding an imperishable phrase in a Harding speech was as unexpected as finding a pearl in a meatball, an event so unlikely that people, including scholars, refused to believe it happened and quickly forgot that it did. The public, usually guided by the press, tends to displace reality with drama and fitness in these matters. What more fitting, historically, than for General John J. Pershing, the most soldierly of soldiers, to step ashore in France at the head of the American Expeditionary Force in World War I and say: "Lafayette, we are here"?

The fact is, though, that the words were spoken as the tag of a speech at Lafayette's tomb in Picpus Cemetery, Paris, on July 4, 1917, by an officer otherwise unknown to fame, a Lieutenant Colonel Charles E. Stanton, the chief disbursing officer for the A.E.F. Similarly, it wasn't Pétain, the defender of Verdun, who said: "*Ils ne passeront pas!*" though it should have been. It was his subordinate, Robert Georges Nivelle, an admirable phrasemaker but a catastrophic general.

The list of famous sayings attributed to the wrong persons is a long one. It was Jefferson, not Washington, who warned against "entangling alliances." It was not Horace Greeley who first trumpeted "Go West, young man!" but J. B. L. Soule, the editor of the Terre Haute *Express*, whose slogan Greeley merely popularized. And it was not Franklin D. Roosevelt who began a speech to the Daughters of the American Revolution with the words "Fellow immigrants. . . ." Though this keeps getting reprinted and will probably never be scotched, it was never uttered. It is, once again, the work of a ghostly unknown who distilled it out of a longer and more labored formulation that F. D. R. used.

With increasingly accurate and instantaneous methods of recording and reproducing speech, the role of the posthumous and retroactive ghost writer, to whom we owe so many of our famous sayings, is diminishing, if not disappearing. In our technological time there is no longer as much possibility for the phraseology of statesmen and leaders to be touched up, altered, and improved once the speech or saying is uttered. In most instances both are firmly cemented into the record at once, just as they are delivered. The ghostwriting must now be done in advance and is generally inferior to the *ex post facto* variety, probably for the same reason that the best lines and wittiest cracks always occur to one after the situation that should have prompted them is past. And freehand invention, no matter how inspired, is no longer possible. Nobody in the future will be able to make up a speech for, say, Dwight D. Eisenhower and get it accepted into the record, as William Wirt did for Patrick Henry or, going farther back in time, as Thucydides did for Pericles in the case of the classic Funeral Oration.

The temper of the time itself is working against the creation of great sayings. Rhetoric and eloquence are out of fashion and are almost everywhere regarded with either suspicion or derision, and usually both. The times being rigidly pragmatic, most men who find themselves in heroic situations make a point of being as hardheaded and unromantic about it as possible. When Edmund Hillary descended from his conquest of Mount Everest in May of 1953, he announced his victory by saying: "We knocked the bastard off." The man who becomes celebrated for daring and high enterprise today is likely to be a skilled technician of some sort, and a flair for language is seldom coupled with technical proficiency. So our astronauts, while performing feats that astound the world, are themselves liable to react with expressions like "Boy, what a ride!" (Alan Shepard) or, if really stirred to their depths, "Man, this is the greatest. Charlie babe, it's fantastic!" (from the Apollo 10 spacecraft).

But the actual landing on the moon, in contrast to the preliminary whirls around it, did produce a memorable saying. It also provided, as an unexpected side effect, a memorable instance of how confusion and misquotation can distort even the most historic remark right at its birth.

Neil Armstrong knew that the whole world would be listening for what he said as he put the first human foot on the lunar surface. He had been prodded on the subject in preflight television interviews. *Esquire* had run several pages of possible sayings by writers and celebrities under the rubric "What Words Should The First Man On the Moon Utter That Will Ring Through The Ages?" A New York radio station had called upon its listeners to submit their own suggestions, and hundreds did. Armstrong would have to deliver something fairly notable or mar the whole mission. It is unlikely that any famous saying in all history was produced under greater pressure than Neil Armstrong's as he stepped from the lunar module at 10:56 P.M. (E.D.T.) on July 20, 1969.

What he said was transmitted instantaneously across more than 200,000 miles of space, was heard by millions, and printed in countless newspapers—incorrectly.

The way his saying was reproduced on the air and in print around the world was: "That's one small step for man, one giant leap for mankind." Hardly anybody seemed to notice that there was something wrong with it. It really didn't make much of a point, since there was no contrast between "man" as used in the saying and "mankind." They both meant the same thing, which left the remark a little flat.

It took Neil Armstrong himself to set the matter right when he got back to earth. Going through the official transcript during his quarantine period, he discovered—no doubt to his horror—that he had been misquoted in every possible medium and language. The line that he must have hoped would ring at least for an age or two was being repeated over and over across the earth with a word missing. The missing word was the smallest one possible in the English language, but its absence ruined his line.

What he had actually said up there on the moon was: "That's one small step for *a* man, one giant leap for mankind."

The indefinite article on which his meaning depended had somehow gotten lost in transmission, probably in static. The *New York Times* subsequently printed Armstrong's revision, and the wire services sent out corrections; but the original and erroneous version will no doubt crop up here and there from now on. It is already embedded in the moon-walk "memorial" issues of the *Times* and other newspapers and is thus irrevocably filed away for the misinformation of future generations.

If astronaut Armstrong's words, even the correct ones, seem somehow inadequate to the stupendous event that prompted them, whose words *would* have been equal to it, short of shooting a Shakespeare into orbit? It may be that we have reached a point where events have outrun man's capacity for responding to them. Once it was possible to get into history, and into the quotation books, by winning a comparatively small naval engagement and announcing: "We have met the enemy and they are ours." That was succinct, it told the story, and

it was equal to the occasion, which was all that was required of a famous saying at that time. But how could anything like it, or anything at all, be equal to what happened on the morning of August 6, 1945, at Hiroshima?

The most lastingly significant occurrence of our time, or of any time, produced no memorable saying; not when it happened and not since, though libraries have been written about it. Captain Robert A. Lewis, who wit-

Edwin Aldrin walks on the face of the moon on July 20, 1969. Samples of a "step for a man" are easily seen, and the man who spoke of them, Neil Armstrong, is reflected in Aldrin's helmet.

nessed it as copilot of the *Enola Gay*, said all that anybody could say under the circumstances. What he said was: "My God!"

Captain Lewis' comment is not much of a coinage, and it does not appear in the quotation books. But it may be the only possible response to most of the major developments of the future.

Richard Hanser is the writer for the National Broadcasting Company's award-winning documentary television series, Project 20. *Among his best-remembered scripts have been* "Meet Mr. Lincoln," "Mark Twain's America," "Meet George Washington," *and, recently,* "The West of Charles Russell."

THE FIRST
TO FLY

By SHERWOOD HARRIS

It seemed, as the year 1903 drew to a close, that man was not quite ready to fly. Many had tried, but so far all had failed to get off the ground in a powered machine that could do more than just return to earth right away. Twice that very year, on October 7 and again on December 8, Charles M. Manly had taken off in self-propelled, gasoline-powered flying machines designed and built by the distinguished head of the Smithsonian Institution, Dr. Samuel Pierpont Langley. Twice Manly had crashed into the Potomac River; twice he had narrowly escaped drowning before managing to free himself from the wreckage. After the second failure the *New York Times* urged Langley to give the whole idea up as a waste of time. "Life is short," the newspaper said, "and his is capable of services to humanity incomparably greater than can be expected to result from trying to fly."

Not all the early test pilots had been as fortunate as the intrepid Manly. The great German glider pilot Otto Lilienthal was dead, his back broken in a glider crash in 1896. And in England, Percy Pilcher, a promising young disciple of Lilienthal's, had also been killed in a glider accident. The others had simply given up when the solution ultimately eluded them.

Then, on December 17, 1903, only nine days after Langley's last failure, came this startling telegram from an obscure sand spit off the North Carolina coast named Kitty Hawk:

SUCCESS FOUR FLIGHTS THURSDAY MORNING ALL AGAINST TWENTY ONE MILE WIND STARTED FROM LEVEL WITH ENGINE POWER ALONE AVERAGE SPEED THROUGH AIR THIRTY ONE MILES LONGEST 57 SECONDS INFORM PRESS HOME CHRISTMAS. OREVELLE WRIGHT

The message was addressed to Bishop Milton Wright of Dayton, Ohio, and it was from his sons Orville—whose name got garbled in transmission—and Wilbur.

The homemade gasoline engine aboard the Wrights' airplane didn't run very well. The aircraft was also hard to control and had a habit of diving abruptly into the sand. It couldn't make a turn yet, much less a precision landing; it was uncomfortable, dangerous, and easily damaged.

But the two shy, strait-laced Wright brothers *were* the first people in the world to achieve powered flight. On December 17 they made four flights—of 120, 175, 180, and 852 feet—and they took photographs to prove it, including perhaps the most dramatic aviation picture of all time (see page 65), showing the first flight just an instant after it became airborne with Orville at the controls.

The first Wright powered machine may have left a lot to be desired as far as performance went, but it was a thing of unique beauty and grace. And in its lines it foreshadowed all that was to follow until man began to send wingless, unstreamlined machines into space. Looking back over sixty years, it may seem that the family resemblance between the Wright machine and today's sleek, modern aircraft is somewhat vague and indistinct. But the resemblance is real enough, for the underlying principles of flight discovered by the Wrights and applied to the design of their aircraft are the same immutable principles that apply today.

With their first flights on December 17, 1903, the Wright

Opposite page: Orville (left) and Wilbur Wright striding down the beach at Kitty Hawk in the fall of 1903 prior to their history-making flights.

brothers demonstrated that they had mastered the three essential elements of flight. First, they had designed wings with sufficient lifting power to sustain their machine in the air. Next, they had built themselves a power plant consisting of engine and propeller that was capable of moving the craft through the air fast enough so that air rushing over the wings generated enough lift to keep the machine airborne. Finally, they had developed a system of controlling the movement of their machine so that once it was off the ground they could keep it off the ground until they were ready to land or—as in the case of the first few flights—until their engine quit.

Others before them, such as Langley, had developed wings with lifting power and power plants capable of driving a machine through the air. In these two areas the Wrights improved substantially on existing technology. But in the field of aircraft control the Wrights, at the very beginning of their interest in flying, came up with a method of controlling the motion of their aircraft that permitted them to succeed where all others had failed. Arguing, debating, discussing things between themselves as the nineteenth century drew to a close, the two brothers made one of those rare intuitive mental leaps that, just when a situation seems stagnant, suddenly sends the human race surging ahead into undreamed-of realms. The Wrights' breakthrough was profound—their control system is used on every fixed-wing aircraft that flies today. And, like most great scientific advances, it was simple. It had to be, for neither brother had gone to college. In fact, neither had finished high school.

Prior to the Wrights the most successful flying machines had been the gliders of Lilienthal in Germany and Octave Chanute in the United States. Between 1891 and 1896 Lilienthal made some two thousand flights in batlike gliders which he launched from a manmade hill near Berlin and controlled by shifting his weight. In some of these he covered distances of nearly one thousand feet. The Chanute glider looked more like a conventional biplane. As in the Lilienthal machine, the pilot dangled below the wings and attempted to control his craft by swinging the lower part of his body. With test pilot A. M. Herring aboard, Chanute tested his designs on the sand hills bordering Lake Michigan near Miller, Indiana, in 1896.

In neither case did control by weight shifting work very well. Lilienthal was fatally injured on a routine flight on August 9, 1896, when a gust of wind threw his glider out of control. Despite the fact that Herring once made a flight of 359 feet in the Chanute machine, experiments with it in the fall of 1896 were generally inconclusive and were soon discontinued.

The problem lay in the fact that a shift of weight—even a large one—was not sufficient to counteract gusts of wind once the Lilienthal and Chanute gliders tipped over beyond a certain point. The balance of these gliders was something like that of a bicycle. As long as they were upright, level, and moving ahead, they were steady. But once they started leaning to one side or the other, they tended to keep right on going over like a leaning bicycle until they passed the point where the shifting of weight would do any good.

The first thing the Wrights did was solve the problem of control. Many years later Orville Wright recalled the chain of events that led to their remarkable piece of deductive reasoning:

"Our first interest began when we were children. Father

brought home to us a small toy actuated by a rubber spring which would lift itself into the air. We built a number of copies of this toy, which flew successfully. . . . But when we undertook to build the toy on a much larger scale it failed to work so well. The reason for this was not understood by us at the time, so we finally abandoned the experiments. In 1896 we read in the daily papers, or in some of the magazines, of the experiments of Otto Lilienthal. . . . His death a few months later . . . increased our interest in the subject and we began looking for books pertaining to flight. We found a work written by Professor [Étienne] Marey on animal mechanism which treated of the bird mechanism as applied to flight, but other than this, so far as I can remember, we found little.

"In the spring of the year 1899 our interest in the subject was again aroused through the reading of a book on ornithology. We could not understand that there was anything about a bird that would enable it to fly that could not be built on a larger scale and used by man. . . . We knew that the Smithsonian Institution had been interested in some work on the problem of flight, and accordingly, on the 30th of May 1899, my brother Wilbur wrote a letter to the Smithsonian inquiring about publications on the subject."

Dr. Langley had done considerable work of his own by this time, had already flown a steam-powered model, and was well up on the work of other people. Thus the Smithsonian sent the Wrights several monographs by Langley as well as papers by Lilienthal, Chanute, and other scientific writers of this period who had explored the problem of flight. The Wrights studied this material and were immediately struck by a fact that everyone else had missed.

They reasoned that if a gust of wind struck a glider and tilted it over to the point of instability, the thing to do was to increase the lift of the low wing so that it would rise, while simultaneously decreasing the lift of the high wing so that it would drop back to a stable level position. This was the breakthrough that was needed. The next step was to figure out a practical way to apply this solution to the control problem. Orville tells how Wilbur worked it out:

"Wilbur . . . demonstrated the method by means of a small pasteboard box, which had two of the opposite ends removed. By holding the top forward corner and rear lower corner of one end of the box between his thumb and forefinger and the rear upper corner and the lower forward corner of the other end of the box in like manner, and by pressing the corners together the upper and lower surface of the box were given a helicoidal twist, presenting the top and bottom surfaces of the box at different angles on the right and left sides. From this it was apparent that the wings of a machine of the Chanute double-deck type, with the fore-and-aft trussing removed, could be warped in like manner so that in flying the wings on the right and left sides could be warped so as to present their surfaces to the air at different angles of incidence and thus secure unequal lifts on the two sides."

That was in late July, 1899. Wilbur was then thirty-two years old and Orville almost twenty-eight. Up until this time they had led serene but somewhat threadbare lives as part of a midwestern minister's large, close-knit family. Bishop Wright was one of the leaders of the United Brethren Church. For al-

most fifty years since his ordination in 1850 he had taught in church schools or preached in a string of small communities in southeastern Indiana. The three older Wright sons—Reuchlin, Lorin, and Wilbur—were all born in Indiana. Orville and his sister Katherine were born in Dayton, where the family had moved in 1869. The Wrights moved back to Indiana once more after that and then settled permanently in Dayton in 1884.

The first time Wilbur and his younger brother Orville teamed up on a major enterprise was in the publication of a Dayton neighborhood newspaper, *The West Side News*, which made its debut in March, 1889. Then, in 1892, sensing the potential of the new "safety" bicycle, the brothers went into the business of selling several well-known makes in Dayton. In their first year in their new enterprise they also added a repair shop to their salesroom. Before long they were manufacturing their own line of bikes, the most popular of which was the Wright Special, which sold for eighteen dollars. As a foundation for the brothers' aeronautical researches, the bicycle business was to prove ideal, for it provided them with the income they needed to support their experiments and a well-equipped machine shop that could turn out just about anything they needed to make an airplane.

The Wrights' first attempt at flight was decidedly casual. A day or two after Wilbur conceived his wing-warping idea, the two brothers began building a large kite to test their new theory. Its design was simple enough: two 5-foot wings were mounted in biplane fashion, one above the other, and were trussed and braced in such a way that they could be warped in the desired fashion by control lines leading to sticks held in either hand. The kite also had a small rigid wooden tail which was supposed to steady it in the air. According to Wilbur's accounts to his family, the model responded very well to the warping control. "We felt," said Orville later, "that the model had demonstrated the efficiency of our system of control."

With this intriguing experience behind them, the brothers began hatching more ambitious plans during the long winter days they spent in the bicycle shop building up their inventory for the heavy spring sales season. "We decided to experiment with a man-carrying machine embodying the principle of lateral control used in the kite model already flown," said Orville. "We expected to fly the machine as a kite and in this way we thought we would be able to stay in the air for hours at a time, getting in this way a maximum of practice with a minimum of effort."

Figuring correctly that a man-carrying kite would require quite a breeze to keep it aloft, the brothers began making inquiries about locations where strong, dependable winds prevailed. After consulting the U.S. Weather Bureau and Octave Chanute, they finally decided upon Kitty Hawk, on the Outer Banks of North Carolina; and on September 6, 1900, Wilbur set out from Dayton, carrying with him all the material needed for a man-carrying glider except some spruce spars which he hoped to purchase en route. Orville planned to follow as soon as the kite was ready to test.

The low, thin sand spits that make up the Outer Banks begin a few miles to the southeast of Norfolk, Virginia, and continue down the North Carolina coast in a meandering line that in places sticks close to the mainland and in others sweeps far out into the ocean. In spots, The Banks are high and wide enough to support sizable towns; in others the beach is barely above water at high tide. The easternmost limit of The Banks is Cape Hatteras, which juts out into the warm water of the Gulf Stream and is so temperate in climate that such southern flora as Spanish moss and scrub palmetto trees flourish there despite the fact that they normally do not occur north of South Carolina. In the summertime, a strong prevailing wind sweeps in off the ocean from the southeast and drives the sand across the dunes in stinging, shifting swirls during the day. When the wind dies down there are mosquitoes.

Arriving at Elizabeth City on the North Carolina coast, Wilbur spent several days trying to book passage to Kitty Hawk, and after a perilous voyage in a leaky fishing boat finally reached the island at nine o'clock in the evening of September 12, more than seven days outbound from Dayton. He boarded at the home of the Kitty Hawk postmaster, William J. Tate, until Orville arrived on September 28. After this the brothers pitched a tent among the dunes.

Almost a year had gone by since Wilbur had tested the controllable kite in Dayton, and the brothers' concept of what the next step should be had undergone an important modification. Instead of simply experimenting further with a larger, man-carrying kite, they planned and built a craft which they hoped would not require a line to hold it into the wind as a kite does, but which would be capable of gliding freely for short distances in a good breeze. And in their thinking they went even beyond this development. A letter from Wilbur to his father, written shortly before Orville arrived in Kitty Hawk, provides the first hint that the brothers had at least considered the problems of powered flight.

"I have my machine nearly finished," Wilbur wrote home. "It is not to have a motor and is not expected to fly in the true sense of the word. My idea is merely to experiment and practice with a view to solving the problem of equilibrium. I have plans which I hope to find much in advance of the methods tried by previous experimenters." He added confidently: "When once a machine is under proper control under all conditions, the motor problem will be quickly solved."

The first Kitty Hawk glider was a biplane design like the Dayton kite and had two 17-foot wings. The ribs of the wings were made of ash and provided a gentle curvature to the upper surfaces; this, the brothers knew from reading about Lilienthal's experiments, would enhance the lifting power of the wings. Both wings were covered with panels of French sateen which had been sewn to size in Dayton ahead of time.

In this early glider, the control problem was not completely solved. The wings and their struts and braces were designed so that they could be warped and the glider tilted, or banked, to counteract any gusts that threatened to upset its equilibrium. But in addition the Wrights anticipated, correctly, that some sort of control would be needed over the up-and-down motion of the craft in order to make the transition between tethered kite and free-flying glider. Once again they rejected the method used by Lilienthal and Chanute of control by shifting the weight of the pilot. Instead, they designed a movable "rudder," which they placed out in front on a separate frame. This rudder (in modern aviation terminology it would be called an elevator) resembled a small wing and when tilted down-

ward tended to force the craft toward the ground. Conversely, when tilted upward it pointed the craft toward the sky.

The forward rudder was operated by a wire which ran back to the center section of the lower wing, where the pilot stretched out on his stomach. As bicycle experts the brothers well knew the value of reducing the amount of air resistance offered by a body sitting upright. Wing warping was also controlled by a wire that led in to where the pilot lay. The brothers quickly discovered when they actually began testing the glider that the pilot couldn't manipulate both wires and still have one hand free to hang on with unless he clenched one of the wires in his teeth. "As we had neither the material nor the tools to change these so as to correct the trouble, we were compelled to test them separately," Wilbur later reported to Octave Chanute in a long, detailed letter. "Two minutes trial was sufficient to prove the efficiency of twisting the planes to obtain lateral balance. We also found our system of fore-and-aft balancing quite effective, but it was only when we came to gliding that we became positive of this."

The new craft was first flown as a kite a few feet off the ground. The brothers conducted several experiments with different loads in different winds and found that it took a fairly stiff breeze of about twenty-five miles per hour to keep their craft in the air with a man aboard. They were somewhat puzzled by the inability of their new wings to generate as much lift as some of Lilienthal's theoretical tables said they should, but their vacation ended on an eminently satisfying note. As Wilbur wrote to Chanute:

"After we found the difficulty of simultaneously maintaining both fore-and-aft and lateral balance we almost gave up the idea of attempting to glide, but just before returning we went down to the big hill which was about three miles from our camp and spent a day in gliding. Our plan of operation was for the aeronaut to lie down on the lower plane while two assistants grasped the ends of the machine and ran forward till the machine was supported on the air. The fore-and-aft equilibrium was in entire control of the rider, but the assistants ran beside the machine and pressed down the end which attempted to rise. We soon found that the machine could soar on a less angle than one in six [a descent of one foot for every six feet of forward motion] and that if the machine was kept close to the slope (which was one in six by measurement) the speed rapidly increased until the runners could no longer keep up. The man on the machine then brought the machine slowly to the ground. . . . We had intended to have the operator turn his body to an upright position before landing but a few preliminary tests having shown that it was feasible to let the machine settle down upon its lower surface with the operator maintaining his recumbent position, we used this method of landing entirely. . . . The distance glided was between three and four hundred feet at an angle of one in six and the speed at landing was more than double that of starting. The wind was blowing about twelve miles. We found no difficulty in maintaining fore-and-aft balance. The ease with which it was accomplished was a matter of great astonishment to us. It was so different from what the writings of other experimenters led us to expect."

Octave Chanute was impressed at Wilbur's report of their successful gliding flights and wrote back a week later to ask

for more details and to get the brothers' permission to use the information they furnished him in a magazine article he was working on. A lively correspondence then ensued between Chanute and Wilbur Wright. Acting as a sounding board, the old engineer drew out the ideas of the brothers, constantly testing and querying and supplying them with information from his own gliding experience and the studies he had made of the works of others, such as Lilienthal. Wilbur, in turn, took full advantage of Chanute's interest and reported on their work and problems at great length in letters that reveal a considerable talent for clarity, interest, and exciting descriptions of the highlights of their experiments.

By the end of October, 1900, the brothers were back in Dayton again. They left their glider behind at Kitty Hawk, where it was soon destroyed by the elements and by Mrs. Tate, wife of the postmaster, who made dresses for her daughters out of the sateen that covered the wings. But this was no great loss; already the Wrights had begun thinking about the next aircraft they would build.

Chanute was graciously included in the brothers' plans for the next session at Kitty Hawk and visited the Wright family in Dayton on June 25 and 26. The return to Kitty Hawk was imminent, and Chanute made arrangements to visit the Wright camp during the summer and to have an experimental machine of his own tested by two protégés, Edward C. Huffaker, who had formerly worked with Langley, and George A. Spratt. On Sunday, July 7, 1901, Wilbur and Orville left together for the Carolina beaches. The trip was much easier this time, and within four days they had begun making a camp at Kill Devil Hills, near Kitty Hawk. The biggest of the dunes there was

about one hundred feet high; it was from this "big hill" that the Wrights had made their successful glider flights just before returning home in 1900.

Since they were expecting company, the Wrights' camp was a bit more elaborate this time. For living quarters, they had a large tent. They also built a wooden shed to house their new glider. "The building is a grand institution, with awnings at both ends; that is, with big doors hinged at the top, which we swing open and prop up," Orville wrote home to his sister Katherine. "We keep both ends open almost all the time and let the breezes have full sway."

But this arrangement left them defenseless against a natural hazard—mosquitoes. On this subject Orville waxed eloquent in his letter to Katherine:

"Mr. Huffaker arrived Thursday afternoon, and with him a swarm of mosquitoes which became a mighty cloud, almost darkening the sun. This was the beginning of the most miserable existence I ever passed through. The agonies of typhoid fever with its attending starvation are as nothing in comparison. But there was no escape. The sand and grass and trees and hills and everything was fairly covered with them. They chewed us clear through our underwear and socks. Lumps began swelling up all over my body like hen's eggs. We attempted to escape by going to bed, which we did at a little after five o'clock. We put our cots out under the awnings and wrapped up in our blankets with only our noses protruding from the folds, thus exposing the least possible surface to attack. Alas! Here nature's complicity in the conspiracy against us became evident. The wind, which until now had been blowing over twenty miles an hour, dropped off entirely. Our blankets then

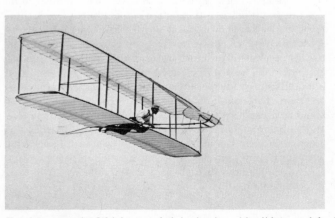

For three years the Wrights tested their theories with gliders; at left above, in 1902, Wilbur is the pilot. Then, in 1903, they were ready for powered flights. Some (above right) fizzled, but on December 17 (opposite page), Wilbur having steadied the wing, Orville was off and flying.

A distinguished contemporary of the Wrights in aviation was Dr. Samuel P. Langley of the Smithsonian Institution. On October 7, 1903, two months before the successful flights at Kitty Hawk, C. M. Manly took off in a Langley-built plane from atop a houseboat on the Potomac, but the plane, reported the Washington Post, *"tumbled over the edge of the houseboat . . . into the river . . . like a handful of mortar." Another take-off, in December, was equally disastrous. Both times, Manly barely escaped.*

became unbearable. The perspiration would roll off us in torrents. We would partly uncover and the mosquitoes would swoop down upon us in vast multitudes. We would make a few desperate and vain slaps, and again retire behind our blankets. Misery! Misery! . . .

"The next night we constructed mosquito frames and nets over our cots, thinking in our childish error we could fix the bloody beasts. We put our cots on the sand twenty or thirty feet from the tent and house, and crawled in under the netting and bedclothes, and lay there on our backs smiling at the way in which we had gotten the best of them. The tops of the canopies were covered with mosquitoes till there was hardly standing room for another one; the buzzing was like that of a mighty buzz saw. But what was our astonishment when in a few minutes we heard a terrific slap and a cry from Mr. Huffaker announcing that the enemy had gained the outer works and he was engaged in a hand-to-hand conflict with them. All our forces were put to complete rout. . . . Affairs had now become so desperate that it began to look as if camp would have to be abandoned or we perish in the attempt to maintain it."

Next they tried building bonfires around the camp, and these helped somewhat, but apparently relief came in a natural way: in a day or two the mosquitoes simply went away. "Yesterday," Orville wrote to Katherine, "most of the mosquitoes had disappeared and we had a fine day and wind for testing the new machine. We took it off to the Big Hill, about a thousand feet distant, and began our experiments. Our first experiments were rather disappointing. The machine refused to act like our machine last year and at times seemed to be entirely beyond our control."

The 1901 glider was similar in design to the aircraft that had been such a success the previous year, but slightly larger. Its biplane wings had a span of twenty-two feet and a total area of roughly three hundred square feet. (The earlier glider had a wingspan of seventeen feet and a total wing area of 165 feet.) The system of control was the same, in principle, as on the earlier craft. Despite its apparent success, the previous year's glider had failed to produce as much lift as Lilienthal's tables indicated it should have; thus the Wrights gave the wings of their 1901 machine a greater curvature to produce a shape more nearly like that used by Lilienthal. All in all, the 1901 glider was a well-built, carefully thought-out aircraft, and it should have performed well.

But it didn't. The first time the brothers tried it out on the big dune at Kill Devil Hills it nosed into the sand after going only a few yards. A second test flight yielded the same results. Believing that there was too much weight forward, the Wrights tried shifting the position of the pilot farther aft for their third attempt. "The machine then sailed off and made an undulating flight of a little more than 300 feet," Wilbur noted. "To the onlookers, this flight seemed very successful, but to the operator it was known that the full power of the rudder had been required to keep the machine from either running into the ground or rising so high as to lose all headway. In the 1900 machine one fourth as much rudder action had been sufficient to give much better control. It was apparent that something was radically wrong, though we were for some time unable to locate the trouble."

The brothers resumed experiments with the machine tethered as a kite in winds of approximately seventeen miles per

hour. Even though they had meticulously designed the wings to correspond with the design used by Lilienthal when he worked out his tables, they found that the lifting power was far less than it should have been. They reasoned that the curvature, or camber, of their wings was too great, despite the fact that it was exactly what Lilienthal recommended. But the Wrights figured that if the top surface of a wing was curved too much, the air flow over the top surface would strike the forward, or leading, edge of the wing at such an angle as to force it down.

So they changed the shape of the wings on their glider and flattened out the curvature of the top surface.

Wilbur wrote:

"On resuming our gliding, we found that the old conditions of the previous year had returned; and after a few trials, made a glide of 389 feet. The machine with its new curvature never failed to respond promptly to even small movements of the rudder. . . . And thereafter we made glide after glide, sometimes following the ground closely, and sometimes sailing high in the air."

The weather turned rainy and unpleasant as the end of August approached, and camp was abandoned; but their experience with the 1901 glider's poor performance in its first few flights made them thoroughly skeptical of the data developed by Lilienthal, and they returned to Dayton determined to run some tests and find out for themselves what kind of wing produced the greatest lift. After experimenting with various testing devices, they finally built a wind tunnel in their Dayton workshop. It was small, measuring six feet in length and having a cross section of sixteen inches square. At one end, a two-bladed fan, driven by a gasoline engine used in their bicycle shop to power a lathe, drill press, and band saw, developed a wind of twenty-five to thirty-five miles per hour. This blast passed through a honeycomb which straightened out the air current generated by the whirling blades of the fan. The wing section to be tested was mounted in the other end of the wind tunnel so that it could move back and forth in the air stream, the amount of movement indicating the amount of lift a particular shape developed. A direct reading of the amount of drag, or resistance to the air flow, was also possible.

The Wright wind tunnel was not the first ever used to test wing shapes, but none had achieved results so spectacular. In their work with their homemade wind tunnel, these two untrained, self-educated engineers demonstrated a gift for pure scientific research that made the more eminent scientists who had studied the problems of flight look almost like bumbling amateurs.

By early October, 1901, the Wrights had their wind tunnel set up and operating well. In the next month they tried out more than one hundred miniature wings of various shapes, including models of bird wings. The letters between Wilbur and Octave Chanute flew thick and fast as Wilbur went into detail on the experiments, and the older man, somewhat doubtful at first, was gradually won over to the Wrights' conviction that previous research on wing design was misleading.

"I am now absolutely certain that Lilienthal's table is very seriously in error, but that the error is not so great as I had previously estimated," Wilbur wrote to Chanute on October 6.

The Wrights emerged from this series of experiments with several notebooks full of data, mankind's first good grasp of the complex theoretical formulas required to predict the lifting power and behavior of different types of wings, and a clear idea of which wing designs would work and which ones were useless. As their busy bicycle-manufacturing season wore on, they completed their plans for an improved glider for the next trip to Kitty Hawk.

The brothers arrived at the site of their previous camp on Thursday, August 28, 1902, and began drilling a well and tidying up their old storage shed. They cannibalized their old 1901 glider, which they had left behind in the shed, to make a new and bigger one, with wings that measured 32 feet 1 inch. It was more graceful-looking due to the fact that the wings were narrower. The curvature of the upper surfaces was also much less pronounced than in the previous year's model, as a direct result of the Wrights' wind tunnel experiments; the new glider incorporated the most efficient wing design that they had developed so far. The design of the control system was refined somewhat in order to permit the pilot, again lying prone, to handle everything and still have a hand left over to hang on with. Up-and-down control was once again effected with a forward horizontal "rudder" that could be tilted by working handles jutting back just in front of the pilot. However, the wing-warping wires were led into a wooden cradle which fitted around the pilot's hips as he lay on the lower wing. By moving his hips from side to side he also moved the cradle from side to side and manipulated the wires that warped the wings of the aircraft.

In their last flights in 1901 the Wrights had experienced some difficulty with the glider's tendency to slew around when the wing-warping controls were used. Now they reasoned that the addition of a fixed vertical tail would stabilize the aircraft when the wings were banked. It did, but a new problem had developed: every time the glider got into a steep bank, its nose pitched up.

After one potentially disastrous crash, which reduced their craft to what Orville described as "a heap of flying machine, cloth, and sticks . . . with me in the center without a bruise or a scratch," Orville had an inspired thought. Why not make the vertical tail movable, instead of fixed? He noted, simply, in his diary: "While lying awake last night, I studied out a new vertical rudder." The Wrights rebuilt their machine, and as October, 1902, drew to a close they made more than 375 flights, including their best: a breathtaking flight of 622½ feet that lasted twenty-six seconds. Control was no longer a problem; the wings they had designed on the basis of scientific data from their wind tunnel experiments proved to be powerful lifting surfaces, and time and time again they soared out from the top of the big hill.

Orville wrote home to Katherine:

"The past five days have been the most satisfactory for gliding that we have had. In two days we made over 250 glides. . . . We have gained considerable proficiency in the handling of the machine now, so that we are able to take it out in any kind of weather. Day before yesterday we had a wind of sixteen meters per second or about 30 miles per hour, and glided in it without any trouble. That was the highest wind a gliding machine was ever in, so that we now hold all the records! The largest machine we handled in any kind of weather, made the longest distance glide (American), the longest time in the air, the smallest angle of descent, and the highest wind!!! Well, I'll leave the rest of the 'blow' till we get home. . . ."

Now all the Wrights needed to do was obtain a lightweight engine, hook it up to a set of propellers, and, in addition to the other records Orville was so proud of, they would have the world's first self-propelled aircraft. In all the world, no one had yet come as close to attaining man's age-old desire to fly as these two self-taught scientists. There had been a flurry of activity in France at about the same time the Wrights began their glider work, but it was not related to the experiments at Kitty Hawk and had been spectacularly unsuccessful. In the United States, Langley was moving steadily and happily toward the disasters of 1903, completely in the dark, as was everyone except Octave Chanute and the Wrights' immediate family, about the significance of the developments on the remote North Carolina beach.

Within a few weeks after their return to Dayton the Wrights began trying to locate a small engine, weighing around 180 pounds, that might develop eight or nine horsepower. They wrote to at least ten well-known American engine manufacturers, but nothing promising turned up. So the brothers decided to build their own engine, counting heavily on the skill and ingenuity of Charles E. Taylor, the top mechanic in their bicycle factory. Here, in Taylor's words, is the way they went about it:

"The first thing we did as an experiment was to construct a sort of skeleton model in order that we might watch the functioning of the various vital parts before venturing with anything more substantial. . . .

"When we had the skeleton motor set up we hooked it up to our shop power, smeared the cylinder with a paint brush dipped in oil and watched the various parts in action. It looked good so we went ahead immediately with the construction of a four cylinder engine. I cut the crank shaft from a solid block of steel weighing over a hundred pounds. When finished it weighed about 19 pounds. We didn't have spark plugs but used the old 'make and break' system of ignition [in which a spark is produced by the opening and closing of contact points inside the combustion chamber]. The gas pump was geared on to the cam shaft and the gas was led in and made to spread over the chamber above the heated water jackets and this immediately vaporized it. . . . I must admit there wasn't much to that first motor—no carburetor, no spark plugs, not much of anything but cylinders, pistons and connecting rods, but it worked." By May of 1903 they had an engine that tested successfully.

Meanwhile, they went to work on the ribs and spars for the wings of their next machine. They had already decided to make it bigger than anything they had tried before. The wings were to be 40 feet 4 inches long and 6 feet 6 inches wide. Instead of making the larger wing ribs out of one solid piece of wood they made them out of two thin strips with the long spars sandwiched in between in order to save weight. They also conducted wind tunnel experiments to see what shape they should use for the struts and braces to cut drag to a minimum. To their surprise a square cross section with the corners slightly rounded off proved to be the design that would slow down their aircraft the least.

Propellers to drive the new craft were expected to present little trouble. Since 1816, when the British experimenter Sir George Cayley thought of the idea of using them on steerable balloons, propellers had become part of the design of every powered aircraft, fanciful and otherwise, that had been seriously advanced, except for the flapping wing, or ornithopter, variety. The only difficulty was that none of the Wrights' predecessors, including Langley, seemed to understand what the problems were when they designed their propellers. Consequently, the Wrights soon discovered that all the previous designs were little more than windmills of various sizes and shapes that beat the air ineffectually, generating little thrust, or pull, despite the horsepower that made them turn. Again they were forced to work out a theory of their own.

From the first the Wrights realized something that previous experimenters had missed. For decades seagoing ships had been pushed through the water by the action of the rear surfaces of their propellers shoving the water behind them. But the Wrights reasoned that aircraft propellers would have to behave differently. They felt that the propeller should be designed like a set of whirling wings in which the forward surface, like the top surface of a wing, developed lift—or in this case, thrust—along the aircraft's flight path.

This piece of reasoning was every bit as important as the thinking that had produced the wing-warping idea and the movable rudder concept of 1902. But the Wrights were in a hurry now. There was much to do before the next summer and too little time to devote to recording the mental process by which they grasped a fact that had eluded many others. So they simply jotted down in a notebook the results of two tests, worked out a formula on the basis of this data that enabled them to predict propeller performance with amazing accuracy, and then made themselves a pair of propellers consisting of three pieces of carved spruce laminated with glue. Rough shaping was done with a hatchet. The brothers used a drawknife to whittle the blades to the final degree of precision.

It was almost the end of September before all was packed up and ready for the return to Kitty Hawk. The Wrights were aware from the newspapers that Langley was about to make his first attempt at flight with his big man-carrying machine, but they weren't particularly concerned. Earlier, Wilbur had even expressed some doubt that the Langley machine would work. "Prof. Langley seems to be having rather more than his share of trouble just now with pestiferous reporters and windstorms," he commented in a letter to Chanute. "It would be interesting to attempt a computation of the possible performance of his machine in advance of his trial, but the data of the machine as given in the newspapers are so evidently erroneous that it seems hopeless to attempt it. . . ."

As October wore on at Kill Devil Hills, the clear days and steady winds prevailed that were ideal for glider flights with the 1902 machine. Instead of going for distance, the Wrights added a new twist to their glider work and began trying to see how long they could remain airborne by "soaring." By this they meant taking off into a wind strong enough to sustain them in a hovering position a few feet from their point of take-off. In previous summers at Kitty Hawk they had marvelled at the ability of buzzards and hawks to do this and had spent many hours watching them hover almost motionless above the dunes. Orville finally set the record with a flight of 1 minute 11⁴/₅ seconds. This, of course, was a world record —and one which stood unchallenged until October 24, 1911, when Orville again broke the record, with a soaring flight of 9³/₄ minutes. The 1911 record was not broken for ten years.

Meanwhile, the new aircraft that would soon change history was beginning to take shape. By October 15, with the assistance of their friend George Spratt, the Wrights had completed the upper wing and covered it with cloth. Another friend sent them a sobering account of Langley's first disastrous attempt at a man-carrying flight, and Wilbur commented in a letter to Chanute: "I see that Langley has had his fling and failed. It seems our luck to throw now, and I wonder what our luck will be."

The transition from glider to powered flying machine was a tremendous step; the 1903 airplane reflected this in almost every detail. The pilot was still going to lie prone on the bottom wing, but when he was stretched out like this, the only place for the engine was to one side of him. However, the engine weighed thirty-four pounds more than either potential pilot; thus the airplane was unbalanced. The Wrights corrected this by adding four inches more to the wing on the heavy side to create additional lift.

Instead of a single propeller, the brothers decided to use a pair of them rotating in opposite directions. For in addition to producing thrust, a whirling propeller also produces torque, a twisting force that tends to pull an airplane to one side. The Wrights figured correctly that they could cancel out this sidewise pull by mounting two propellers that would turn, and thus pull, in opposite directions. Connecting the propellers to the engine was a chain-and-sprocket drive—the only feature on the machine that betrayed its humble bicycle-shop origin.

As in the 1902 glider, a hip cradle controlled the warping of the wings and caused the aircraft to bank. The movable tail was also connected to the hip cradle. The front horizontal rudder, which made the plane climb and dive, was once again controlled by a wire that ran back to a lever within reach of the pilot. The engine was essentially uncontrollable. Once it was started and adjusted on the ground, the only thing the pilot could do to it was to stop it by pulling on a lever that interrupted the ignition.

The lower wing, rudder, and tail surfaces were completed toward the end of October, and most of the uprights and wire braces had been installed between the two wings. On November 2 the Wrights began hooking up the engine and the propellers. Two days later Orville optimistically noted in his diary: "Have machine now within half day of completion." But now, after such a long period of success, they ran into a frustrating series of setbacks.

First, two propellers came loose on their shafts the first time the engine was started up. The shafts were sent via Spratt back to Charley Taylor in Dayton. The new shafts arrived on November 20. This time the sprockets for the chain drives from the engine began to slip. No amount of tightening seemed to help. In desperation the two men turned to a tire cement

known as Arnstein's, which Orville claimed would fix anything from a stop watch to a threshing machine. It must have been a remarkable compound, for after they had filled the threads of the sprocket screws with Arnstein's and let it set awhile, they had no more difficulty with loose sprockets.

On November 25, just as the brothers were getting ready to take the new machine out for their first trial flight, it began to rain. Before the skies cleared up again, a crack developed in one of the propeller shafts. Orville left for Dayton on November 30 to make new and, he hoped, foolproof shafts. He arrived back at the camp on Friday, December 11. The shafts were installed, and the machine was hauled out on Saturday for another attempt at flight, but the brothers judged that there was not sufficient wind to take off from the level ground right near their camp and not enough time to try for a launching down the big hill, almost half a mile away. The next day the weather was perfect, but it was Sunday, and that, to the bishop's sons, meant no flying.

The Wrights' activities in four seasons at Kitty Hawk had generated considerable interest among the few residents there. The brothers had consequently acquired a set of loyal fans who didn't want to miss the final act. They arranged to hoist a signal on a small flagstaff when they were about to make their first attempt at flight so that the men at the Kill Devil Hills lifesaving station just about a mile away would have enough notice to walk over in time for the attempt.

At half past one on the afternoon of Monday, December 14, the Wrights hoisted their signal and started walking their machine toward the big hill. There they were met by six men from the lifesaving station, who helped them lug the 605-pound aircraft to the top. The brothers tossed a coin to decide who was to go first, and Wilbur won.

Since the new plane was so heavy—the 1902 glider had weighed only 112 pounds—the Wrights were concerned about the possibility that its skids would dig into the sand during the take-off run and prevent a lift-off. So they built a sixty-foot wooden track made of four 15-foot two-by-fours placed end to end on the sand. To the top surface they nailed a metal strip. A small wooden dolly or "truck" ran along this track on two rollers made from bicycle hubs. The sledlike skids of the aircraft rested on this dolly.

Unfortunately the attempt on Monday, with Wilbur at the controls, was a flop. "The machine turned up in front and rose to a height of about 15 feet from ground at a point somewhere in the neighborhood of 60 feet from end of track," Orville wrote. "After thus losing most of its headway it gradually sank to the ground turned up at an angle of probably 20° incidence."

Some early aviators might have been tempted to call this first sixty-foot hop a "flight," but not the Wrights. However, they were now confident of ultimate success. They got off a telegram to their father telling him, "Success assured keep quiet."

It took them a day to repair the damaged plane. Then the weather failed to co-operate again. Thursday, December 17, was perfect for flying, though seasonably cold. The wind was blowing from the north at twenty to twenty-five miles an hour, and the puddles near camp were covered with ice. The two brothers waited awhile to see whether the wind would hold. By this time they had been at their camp eighty-four days, their food was mostly beans, and it was beginning to be bitterly cold. But they knew their machine would work. So they hoisted their signal and were soon joined by several men from the lifesaving station. They must have been moved by an uncanny sense of history that morning, for they painstakingly adjusted their cumbersome glass-plate camera so that it could snap a picture at the precise moment of lift-off.

Again Orville's diary preserves the flavor of the historic occasion:

"After running the engine and propellers a few minutes to get them in working order, I got on the machine at 10:35 for the first trial. The wind . . . was blowing . . . 27 miles [per hour] according to the Government anemometer at Kitty Hawk. On slipping the rope the machine started off increasing speed to probably 7 or 8 miles. The machine lifted from the truck just as it was entering on the fourth rail. Mr. Daniels [from the Kill Devil Hill Life Saving Station] took a picture just as it left the tracks. I found the control of the front rudder quite difficult on account of its being balanced too near the center and thus [it] had a tendency to turn itself when started so that the rudder was turned too far on one side and then too far on the other. As a result the machine would rise suddenly to about 10 ft. and then as suddenly, on turning the rudder, dart for the ground. A sudden dart when out about 100 feet from the tracks ended the flight. Time about 12 seconds (not known exactly as watch was not promptly stopped). . . ."

Then it was Wilbur's turn again. Orville continues his narrative:

"After repairs, at 20 min. after 11 o'clock Will made the second trial. The course was like mine, up and down but a little longer over the ground though about the same in time. Dist. not measured but about 175 ft. Wind speed not quite so strong. With the aid of the station men present, we picked the machine up and carried it back to the starting ways. At about 20 minutes till 12 o'clock I made the third trial. When out about the same distance as Will's, I met with a strong gust from the left which raised the left wing and sidled the machine off to the right in a lively manner. I immediately turned the rudder to bring the machine down and then worked the end control. Much to our surprise, on reaching the ground the left wing struck first, showing the lateral control of this machine much more effective than on any of our former ones. At the time of its sidling it had raised to a height of probably 12 to 14 feet.''

This is Orville's triumphant telegram to his father in Dayton, announcing the first successful flights. Western Union got his name wrong.

The third flight was a short hop by Orville. The fourth and last flight, made by Wilbur, was the most spectacular and satisfying of all. Again Orville describes it in his diary:

"At just 12 o'clock Will started on the fourth and last trip. The machine started off with its ups and downs as it had done before, but by the time he had gone over three or four hundred feet he had it under much better control, and was traveling on a fairly even course. It proceeded in this manner till it reached a small hummock out about 800 feet from the starting ways, when it began its pitching again and suddenly darted into the ground. The front rudder frame was badly broken up, but the main frame suffered none at all. The distance over the ground was 852 feet in 59 seconds. The engine turns was 1071, but this included several seconds while on the starting ways and probably about half a second after landing. The jar of landing set the watch on the machine back so that we have no exact record for the 1071 turns. Will took a picture of my third flight just before the gust struck the machine. The machine left the ways successfully at every trial, and the tail was never caught by the truck as we had feared.

"After removing the front rudder, we carried the machine back to camp. We set the machine down a few feet west of the building and while standing about discussing the last flight, a sudden gust of wind struck the machine and started to turn it over. All rushed to stop it. Will who was near one end ran to the front, but too late to do any good. Mr. Daniels and myself seized the spars at the rear, but to no purpose. The machine gradually turned over on us. Mr. Daniels, having had no experience in handling a machine of this kind, hung onto it from the inside, and as a result was knocked down and turned over and over with it as it went. His escape was miraculous as he was in with the engine and chains. The engine legs were all broken off, the chain guides badly bent, a number of uprights and nearly all the rear ends of the ribs were broken. One spar only was broken."

The historic first successful airplane was never to fly again. The brothers packed it up and brought it back to Dayton with them as they hurried home for Christmas. It was later reassembled and exhibited a couple of times in New York and once at M.I.T. For many years it languished in a shed at Dayton; then, in 1928 it was sent to the Science Museum in London after the Smithsonian Institution refused to recognize it as the first successful airplane, giving Langley's machine that honor. In 1942, after many years of controversy, the Smithsonian belatedly reversed its position, and Orville Wright asked the Science Museum to return the aircraft to the United States when it would be safe to do so after the war. After Orville Wright's death in January, 1948, the 1903 machine came back from twenty years' exile. It was refurbished and placed on exhibit on December 17, 1948, the forty-fifth anniversary of its first flight.

Sherwood Harris is with the International General Books division of the Reader's Digest. *A former Navy carrier pilot who still gets aloft occasionally, he wrote an article called "Coast to Coast in 12 Crashes" for our October, 1964, issue that became the germ of the book from which the foregoing excerpt has been taken. Entitled* The First to Fly: Aviation's Pioneer Days, *Mr. Harris' book will be published this month by Simon & Schuster.*

tioned by Jones, the fishermen declared that the ship he had spotted in the Lough was the *Drake*, a twenty-gun sloop of war that offered just about an even match for the eighteen-gun *Ranger*. The Royal Navy, which supposedly kept the Irish Sea as safe for British shipping as the Thames, was at last showing a representative.

Never one to hesitate when a challenge was in the air,

failed to drop anchor until the *Ranger* had floated beyond her strategic position, Jones found the situation too risky and ordered the cable cut. The *Ranger* fled the scene of this dangerously botched job. Officers and sailors alike, numbering almost 150 altogether, were quite content to assume that the *Drake* would never see them again; but their captain had other ideas.

Gale-force winds came up on Tuesday, the twenty-first, and dashed Jones's hopes of an immediate return to the *Drake*. The seamen spent the day battling the wind and growing more and more displeased with their

Some accounts of Jones's "invasion" of St. Mary's Isle call Lord Selkirk's residence a castle. That it was not, but it was a good, substantial specimen of an English country mansion, and it survived until 1893, when it was demolished to make room for a new house.

Captain Jones "ordered the ship to be put about in order to go in and cut her out," reported Ezra Green, the *Ranger*'s surgeon, in his diary. However, Jones soon learned that his men were not in the mood for such boldness in broad daylight. Instead they agreed on a sneak attack at midnight. The belief shared by nearly everyone on board that the captain's orders should be subject to a majority veto is apparent in Surgeon Green's offhand explanation of this piece of insubordination: "the wind blowing fresh and the people unwilling to undertake it we stood off and on till midnight when the people consenting and the wind having lulled a little we stood into the River [the Lough]. . . ."

Guided through darkness by the captive fishermen, the *Ranger* came within a hundred feet of the *Drake*. However, thanks to an inebriated boatswain's mate who

leader's strategy, which clearly was not designed to make them rich. Meanwhile, Jones made up his mind to strike at Britain herself, instead of just one of her warships. Now he would put his childhood memories to use.

It was from Whitehaven, the busy port on the English coast just below Solway Firth, that thirteen-year-old John Paul had first sailed for America as ship's boy on the brig *Friendship*. And it was Whitehaven that he chose now as his target, because he knew the entry to the harbor as well as he knew his own real name. But when he announced his plan, he found that his enthusiasm had not infected his officers. As the *Ranger* made her way slowly east in a weakening wind, Jones called for volunteers. Lieutenants Simpson and Hall promptly declined on grounds of exhaustion. Some of the officers protested that there was no military excuse for "burning poor people's property." It was true that most of the shipping at Whitehaven consisted of trading vessels and fishing boats. Setting fire to them would not weaken the Royal Navy. But in Jones's eyes the attack would surely justify itself by its propaganda value.

Despite the mutterings of Simpson and Hall and their admirers, Jones was able to muster a party of forty raiders, who would make the landing in two boats. The men volunteered for various reasons, some for adventure, some hoping for plunder, perhaps a few out of loyalty to their captain. One of the volunteers was a

John Paul Jones was born in this cottage at Arbigland, Scotland, about thirty-five miles from the Selkirk estate, on July 6, 1747.

twenty-two-year-old sailor who was listed on the ship's roll as David Smith but whose real name was David Freeman. Like his captain, Freeman had been born in the British Isles; but while John Paul Jones had felt no qualms in transferring his allegiance to America, for Freeman this had proved impossible.

The captain himself was to command the first landing boat, with Lieutenant Meijer as his mate. Meijer was a volunteer from the Swedish Army who distinguished himself among these Americans as the only officer completely loyal to Jones. Lieutenant Wallingford, who headed the *Ranger*'s contingent of marines, would be in charge of the second boat. Each of the raiders was armed with pistol and cutlass. Jones addressed them briefly before they embarked, promising that he would be "the first who landed and the last who left the shore." It was

already midnight when the boats left the *Ranger*, and thanks to weak winds the harbor was still several miles away. The tide was going out, and it was only after three hours of rowing that the Americans stepped onto the English beach. The first pallor of dawn already appeared in the east.

In the meantime the guards stationed in the more southerly of the two forts of Whitehaven, which defended the north and south sides of the harbor, were dozing in the guardhouse. The night was chilly, and they were sure there was no point in standing watch outside. Suddenly they found themselves awake, surrounded by a ring of tough-looking sailors—pirates, the guards must have assumed—with pistols trained on their foreheads. Was it a dream?

Minutes earlier Captain Jones and most of the men of his boat had scaled the walls of the southern fort "by mounting upon the shoulders of our largest and strongest men," as Jones reported. He himself had been the first of the attackers. The English guards "were secured without being hurt," and the Americans quickly spiked all the cannon of the fort. Jones then ran the quarter of a mile to the northern fort and spiked its guns as well, accompanied only by one midshipman. But when the intrepid commander got back to the beach he found that the other raiders had failed to emulate him. He had sent Wallingford's party to burn the vessels on the north side of the harbor, but instead they had broken into a convenient alehouse and helped themselves liberally to its wares. Their explanation as to why they had set fire to nothing other than their own throats was that their torch had burned out. In his official report Jones describes his disappointment with a remarkable lack of rancor:

On my return from this business [spiking the guns], I naturally expected to see the fire of the ships on the north side, as well as to find my own party with every thing in readiness to set fire to the shipping on the south; instead of this, I found the boat under the direction of Mr. Hill and Mr. Wallingford returned, and the party in some confusion, their light having burnt out at the instant when it became necessary. By the strangest fatality, my own party were in the same situation, the candles being all burnt out. The day too came on apace, yet I would by no means retract while any hopes of success remained.

As if Captain Jones did not have enough problems with drunken and mutinous assistants, he also had an out-and-out traitor trying to sabotage the raid. No sooner had David Freeman got out of Jones's sight than he broke away from his party and went dashing along the streets nearest the waterfront, shouting at the top of his lungs that "pirates" were on the beach. The sleepy townfolk at first regarded this English version of Paul Revere as a crazy man, but after a few minutes the alarm was spreading faster than the fire that Jones had hoped to start.

That fire, in fact, had yet to be kindled. Jones was unaware of Freeman's performance, but he saw the townsfolk gathering near the wharves. Undaunted, he picked out one of the 150 or more ships grounded on the beach, a coal carrier named *Thompson*, and sent a man aboard her with a torch, having gotten a light in a house nearby. Jones's account of the scene is typically well phrased:

I should have kindled fires in other places if the time had permitted; as it did not, our care was to prevent the one kindled from being easily extinguished. After some search a barrel of tar was found, and poured into the flames, which now ascended from all the hatchways. The inhabitants began to appear in thousands, and individuals ran hastily towards us. I stood between them and the ship on fire, with a pistol in my hand, and ordered them to retire, which they did with precipitation. The flames had already caught in the rigging, and began to ascend the mainmast; the sun was a full hour's march above the horizon, and as sleep no longer ruled the world, it was time to retire.

Jones took care to make his escape appear as fearless as his arrival. True to his word, the captain was the last man into the boat, delaying a few moments "to observe at my leisure the terror, panic, and stupidity of the inhabitants." Jones might have omitted this piece of bravado had he known that it was only due to the unflinching loyalty of Lieutenant Meijer that his crew had not rowed away without him.

On their way out of the harbor the boats were fired on by a few cannons that the raiders had neglected to spike. But the shooting was so pitifully wide of the mark that Jones's men found it amusing rather than frightening, and returned the "salute" with a few good-natured pistol shots. The *Ranger* had sailed closer, and the boats reached her about 6 A.M. Jones had freed all the prisoners taken at the forts except three, whom he kept "as a *sample*."

Thus concluded America's brief invasion of England, if such it may be called. Of course, Jones never contemplated marching inland at the head of his tiny "army." But on the morning of April 23, 1778, and for months thereafter, few natives of Whitehaven could believe that their town had not been invaded by an invincible force commanded by an evil genius named John Paul Jones. The London *Gazetteer and New Daily Advertiser* commented sarcastically:

The people of Whitehaven, it is thought, can never recover from their fright; two thirds of the people are bordering on *insanity;* the remainder on *idiotism;* the defence of the harbour is left to the care of the old women, who declare that had they been called into power earlier, they would have preserved the town with their *mopsticks* and cut off the retreat of the rebels.

The fire on the *Thompson* had been brought under control quickly enough to keep it from spreading to other ships, but the panic that Jones had inspired, and that he took such pleasure in observing, was not so easily extinguished. It swept along the British coast and set thousands of villagers to scanning the horizon daily; insurance rates increased 300 per cent on shipping to Ireland. Moreover, the Royal Navy was sorely embarrassed by charges of extreme negligence. And the name of the "provincial privateer" who had caused all the furor was on its way to fame.

As he returned to his ship, however, Jones was not congratulating himself on winning notoriety. In his view the Whitehaven operation had been a fiasco. There had been no conflagration, and now every English seaport would be on the lookout. And the disaffection of his crew did not bode well for future operations. Ignorant of David Freeman's contribution to the night's events, Jones could only blame the failure on the lateness of the landing and "the backwardness of some persons under my command." In his report to Congress, Jones expressed nostalgia for the reliable officers who had served him in his two earlier Navy commands, the *Providence* and the *Alfred:* "had they been with me in the *Ranger* 250 or 300 sail of large ships at Whitehaven would have been laid in ashes."

And so, on the morning of April 23, this uncommon commander felt a need to strike again, to offset the negative results of the past night; and he knew there was little time before news of his attack would spread. Moreover, he was anxious to do something about the matter of prisoner exchanges. So he turned the *Ranger* northwest, toward St. Mary's Isle, with a very unorthodox end in view.

Just four hours after leaving Whitehaven the Americans arrived at Kirkcudbright Bay. Taking fourteen men, Jones got into the *Ranger's* cutter and guided it through the shallow channel that he had learned to follow as a twelve-year-old sailor and as a twenty-one-year-old trader. By about 11 A.M. the cutter pulled up on the nearest shore of the tiny peninsula that was St. Mary's Isle. Accompanied by crew master David Cullam, Lieutenant Wallingford, and the seamen, all equipped with pistol and cutlass, Captain Jones strode up the path through the woods toward the Earl of Selkirk's mansion. On the way the group met and questioned a few of the Earl's hired hands, brusquely announcing themselves to be a Royal Navy press gang hunting for "volunteers." The effect of this news was to send all the able-bodied workers of the estate hurrying off to Kirkcudbright, since none of them was eager to swab the decks of a British frigate. One of the gardeners, however, gave Jones a piece of news in return that was even less happily received: "The Earl is not at home." On hearing this the captain glumly turned his steps back toward his boat.

Lady Selkirk's elegant silver teapot still belongs to the Selkirk family. The rest of the "plate" taken by Jones's men, and later returned by him, has long since been sold.

For the temerarious aim of his visit had been to kidnap the Earl and hold him as a hostage for the release of American naval prisoners.

This outlandish scheme has given rise to much speculation and mythmaking about Jones's "real" purpose in going after Lord Selkirk. The latter may have been the foremost citizen of his area, but he had nothing whatever to do with London's war policy; King George barely knew he existed. Thus Jones's mythologizers have cast about to discover a clue to the would-be kidnapper's ulterior motive, and many have claimed to find it in the doubts that persist about John Paul's parentage. There is no real evidence that he was not the son of John Paul, Sr., gardener of the estate of Arbigland. But many writers have been eager to believe that John Paul was a bastard son of Lord Selkirk, or at least that he believed himself to be, and that he came to St. Mary's to get revenge on the father who had abandoned him. Like many other legends, this one is founded solely on the lack of absolute proof that it is false. The most plausible explanation of Jones's rather foolish kidnapping plan is that the importance of Lord Selkirk had been vastly exaggerated in John Paul's youthful mind and that in his absence from Britain Jones had never relieved himself of this illusion.

No wonder, then, that the captain was crestfallen when he heard that the Earl was away, and was anxious to leave the scene of his second disappointment of the morning. But now Cullam and Wallingford interrupted his thoughts, saying it was crazy to pass up the chance to rob a defenseless mansion belonging to the enemy. They reminded Jones of the crew's resentment over his refusal to make plunder the chief object of the voyage; they also complained that "in America, no delicacy was shown by the English, who took away all sorts of movable property."

Hoping no doubt to win some sorely needed popularity with his men, Jones agreed to let the two officers enter the mansion and take the family silver, on condition that they leave the sailors outdoors, injure no one, and satisfy themselves with whatever valuables were freely turned over to them. Cullam and Wallingford agreed and led the sailors toward the house while Jones returned to the cutter to wait.

The house that the two officers directed the sailors to surround was not a castle, as some wishful writers have called it, but a handsome old mansion with a high roof and wide yards. Inside there were no men of the family to meet the two strangers at the door; there were only the Countess, her children, servants, and four female guests. But it soon became clear that the Countess needed no one to help her handle the intruders. She acted throughout as if she knew that her conduct would some day be described by historians. When Cullam, a hard-bitten rogue, demanded the silver and growled, "It is needless to resist," she answered calmly, "I am very sensible of that."

In order to avoid violence, and because of her inbred distaste for deception, Lady Selkirk chose to co-operate completely. She caught old Daniel trying to hide some of the silver plate in a maid's apron, reprimanded him, and submitted all there was in the pantry to the Americans who, she later wrote, "very deliberately called for sacks to put everything up." The Countess even gave Cullam an inventory of the house's silver, which prompted him to demand her teapot and coffeepot. The teapot came complete with the breakfast tea leaves still in the bottom. As these transactions were going on, the Countess was impressed by the demeanor of Lieutenant Wallingford, who seemed to regret the discomfort they had caused her. She offered a glass of wine to both Americans, which they accepted. By now, however, they were anxious to get away, and with good reason, since a group of local stalwarts were on their way from Kirkcudbright to repulse the "invaders." Carrying their small treasure, Cullam and Wallingford marched their troop back to the shore, got in the boat with Captain Jones, and rowed out to the *Ranger*. It was in this rather unglorious way that the United States Navy departed Scotland with the spoils of war. The whole affair had lasted about twenty minutes.

They must have been a nervous twenty minutes for the captain, who didn't relish the prospect of being labelled a common thief. From Wallingford he extracted a full report on the scene at the house, and the story of Lady Selkirk's aplomb inspired in Jones a great respect for her, which was to manifest itself effusively. He resolved to buy the silver with his own funds when his crew sold it as booty, and return it to this splendid female. The impetus behind this resolve was not merely a respect for private property nor the appreciative courtesy of a connoisseur of women. Ever alert for opportunities to cut a heroic figure in the eyes of persons of high station, the indefatigable captain was already hoping, we are entitled to suspect, that his ignominious robbery would open the door to an applause-winning gesture of chivalry. By the time the *Ranger* got back to France, Jones had spent a good deal of time in his cabin working on one of the best letters ever produced by his suave pen. He sent this letter to Lady Selkirk from Brest on May 8, the day of his arrival there.

But before Jones could employ his genius as a writer, there was the problem of proving his genius as a fighter. By noon on the day of Lord Selkirk's nonabduction, the *Ranger* was sailing toward Ireland and her commander was shoving thoughts of the Lord's wife to the back of his mind. Twice he had landed on enemy territory, but he had no military achievement to show for it. All he had done was to stir up a lot of British villagers. "There are more men under arms," Lady Selkirk wrote to her sister on the afternoon of April 23, "than I thought there were men or arms in this quarter." The volunteer guardsmen of Kirkcudbright had hauled a rusty old cannon to the shore, and that night they repeatedly fired salvos at what looked like a ship in the bay. According to one of Jones's early biographers, Alexander Mackenzie:

When the day dawned, the valiant burghers were overwhelmed with mortification at discovering, that they had been venting their prowess upon an invulnerable rock which stood at no great distance from the land.

Had he known about this barrage, John Paul Jones would not have been overly amused. By now he was desperate for some real action in which he could win the recognition that the Continental Congress had so far failed to give him. He thought of H.M.S. *Drake*. The *Ranger* headed for Belfast Lough.

The sun was just coming up on April 24, 1778, when the *Drake*'s lookout spotted an unfamiliar sail approaching the harbor. The *Ranger* was still masquerading as a merchantman, so presently the *Drake*'s elderly commander, Captain John Burden, sent a boat to identify the stranger. In the meantime the animosity felt by the American crew toward their ambitious leader was boiling over; led by the vituperative Lieutenant Simpson they were below decks, debating whether they should refuse to fight. When they heard that a defenseless British boat was coming close, some of them went up to watch how Captain Jones would handle the Royal Navy's emissary. It was a good show. The British officer commanding the rowboat lifted his spyglass again and again to get a side view of the *Ranger* and ascertain whether she carried cannon. But Jones tacked so skillfully as to show only the *Ranger*'s stern to the spyglass; the officer had to come alongside and board in order to learn the ship's identity. This was imparted together with the further information that he and his five oarsmen and their boat had just been captured by John Paul Jones. Those seamen of the *Ranger* who had watched this excellent trick performed were quick to tell their shipmates, and all hands were so pleased by Jones's cunning that mutiny was forgotten.

The *Drake*, getting no response to her signals for recall of her boat, hauled anchor and began to sail out of the harbor. Jones withdrew until the other ship was well away from shore, then waited. The breeze was light, and it was not until almost 6 P.M. that the *Drake* hailed her adversary, who had lured her all the way to the middle of the North Channel. Then for the first time the *Ranger* hoisted the Stars and Stripes. Surgeon Green recorded

FRANCIS AND SHAW

SCOTLAND

✠ Engagement With H.M.S. Drake
St. Mary's Isle, Kirkcudbright
Belfast
Whitehaven (Raid)

IRELAND

ENGLAND

London

ENGLISH CHANNEL

FRANCE

Brest

RANGER'S CRUISE AROUND IRELAND 1778

QUIBERON BAY
(First salute to U.S. flag)

the suddenness with which Jones began the battle: "after the usual Compliments were pass'd we wore Ship & gave her a whole broadside, without receiving a Shot."

Probably right up until the very last minute Captain Burden had been hoping that the stranger would flee or surrender without a fight. After the battle the London *Advertiser* tried to explain his lack of fervor by pointing out that he was "in years, and at that time very ill." Burden's men, however, fought fiercely. The two sloops of war were fairly matched. The *Drake* carried twenty cannons firing six-pound shot; the *Ranger* had eighteen nine-pounders. Perhaps 175 men were on the *Drake*, some of them volunteers from Belfast who had come aboard when they heard an American raider was nearby. Jones's crew numbered less than 130 now, having lost several prize crews to take over earlier captures. Mackenzie may have a point in claiming that the British had a psychological advantage:

. . . the *Drake* belonged to a regularly established navy, whose ships were everywhere accustomed to conquer, whilst the equipping of the *Ranger* was among the earliest efforts of a new and imperfectly organized service.

But when Jones's New Englanders were in the mood to fight, as they were now, victorious traditions were of little help to the men of H.M.S. *Drake*.

After the *Ranger*'s opening broadside the two ships blasted away at each other for an hour and five minutes. The laconic Dr. Green described the action as "very warm." At one point Jones saw that his gunners were firing mainly when the side of the ship was rolling down in the trough of the waves. They explained this was in order to drop their cannon balls low into the *Drake*'s hull and sink her. But Jones had gone long enough with nothing to show for his daring stratagems—he wanted to keep the *Drake* afloat as a prize. So his gunners, following his instructions, began firing on the upward roll of the ship in order to tear up the enemy's rigging. Their aim was accurate. Jones was later willing to pay them a high compliment despite their disloyal tendencies: "They gave the *Drake* three broadsides for two right along at that. . . . My supply of ammunition would never admit of actual target practice, so the precision of their fire was simply natural aptitude."

When the battle had gone on without letup for at least an hour, Captain Burden was struck in the head by a musket ball fired by one of Wallingford's marines from the *Ranger*'s maintop. Almost at the same time his second officer, Lieutenant Dobbs, was mortally wounded. With sails utterly in shreds and the crew in desperate confusion, the *Drake*'s third-in-command saw no choice but to shout the signal for surrender. In the captured boat from the *Drake* a group of Americans crossed to the maimed

vessel and disarmed the English crew. The *Ranger* took the *Drake* in tow.

As the sun set over Ireland, at least seven men lay dead or dying. Three Americans had been killed in the maintop by British sharpshooters. One of these was Lieutenant Wallingford, who had made such a good impression on Lady Selkirk. In June her husband the Earl mentioned Wallingford in his reply to Jones's letter to the Countess:

We were all sorry to hear afterwards that the younger officer in green uniform [the color of the marines] was killed in your engagement with the *Drake*, for he in particular showed so much civility and so apparent dislike at the business he was then on [taking the silver], that it is surprising how he should have been one of the proposers of it.

In addition to the deaths of Wallingford and two seamen, five Americans were wounded, while the British reported nineteen wounded. Jones later asserted that the number of enemy wounded was closer to forty.

The record reveals some poignant details. At the time of his death Lieutenant Wallingford had a son two months old. Lieutenant Dobbs of the *Drake*, who died of his wound thirty-six hours after the fight, had been married three days before. Old Captain Burden lived long enough to be aware that he had lost his ship, and then succumbed to his head wound. Surgeon Green listed the wounded Americans: ". . . Pierce Powers lost his right Hand, & his left badly wounded. James Falls by a musket shot through the Shoulder. Tho.s Taylor lost his little Finger by a musket shot at the wheel."

Captain Jones sincerely regretted the loss of life and limb caused by his victory. He meant it when he wrote, "Humanity starts back from such scenes of horror." At the same time, though, he had reason to be proud. His men had fought bravely, but the main credit for victory unquestionably belonged to Jones. He had overcome both their disloyalty and the valor of the prestigious enemy by his brilliant tactics and determination to win. The victory had converted the *Ranger*'s cruise into a military triumph after a series of colorful but disappointing enterprises. Never before had an American defeated a British warship in all-out, one-to-one combat. That Jones's spirits were uplifted is shown by a flippant gesture that made him a kind of Robin Hood to the villagers of eastern Ireland. The day after the battle Jones set free the fishermen captured on the twentieth, giving them the *Drake*'s boat and a present of fifteen guineas for their trip home. According to a local newspaper, "He also gave them a piece of the Drake's mainsail, which was very much shattered, desiring them to carry it to the Governor of Carrickfergus . . . and to tell him he had sent it to make him a pair of trousers."

Yet when Jones reached France he was not universally acclaimed. His progress toward fame had always been hindered by his lack of family connections and political pull. It seemed to him that everyone except his friends persisted in ignoring him. Another year and another ship would have to come before John Paul Jones was recognized as a national hero. But the future commander of the *Bonhomme Richard* had learned a good deal during his exploits with U.S.S. *Ranger*; and in the course of them he had revealed many of the traits in his intricate personality.

Even more about his personality comes to light, however, in the epistolary tour de force that Lady Selkirk received, to her great surprise, in early June. The letter begins by assuring the Countess that the loss of her silver distressed Jones as much as her. Jones describes himself as an "Officer of fine feelings and of real Sensibility." He justifies having permitted his men to go after the silver on the grounds that British soldiers had committed atrocities in New England that made the men of the *Ranger* feel obligated to retaliate somehow. However, Jones declares, he gave Cullam and Wallingford firm orders to treat the Countess "with the utmost Respect." He promises, moreover, that "when the plate is sold, I shall become the Purchaser, and I will gratify *my own feelings* by restoring it to you, by such conveyance as you shall be pleased to direct."

Jones goes on to relate his victory over the *Drake*, thinking, perhaps, to overawe milady with images of "the awful Pomp and dreadful Carnage of a Sea Engagement." Responsibility for "this detested War," Lady Selkirk is assured, lies with Britain for having infringed on "the rights of men." Therefore: "As the feelings of your gentle Bosom cannot but be congenial with mine—let me entreat you Madam to use your soft persuasive Arts with your Husband to endeavor to stop this Cruel and destructive War, in which Britain can never succeed."

This charming missive mattered so much to its author that he eventually sent the Countess three separate original copies, as well as making copies for various people whose esteem he wished to keep, including Benjamin Franklin in Paris. The old doctor gave it a good review: "a gallant letter, which must give her ladyship a high opinion of his generosity and nobleness of mind." The letter's outspoken quality notwithstanding, Jones's motives in writing it are less than trans-

Mark Halliday is a student at Brown University.

For further reading: John Paul Jones: A Sailor's Biography, *by Samuel Eliot Morison (Little, Brown, 1959);* John Paul Jones, Fighter for Freedom and Glory, *by Lincoln Lorenz (United States Naval Institute, 1943).*

parent. The egotism with which he had always approached his notoriously successful romantic liaisons may have persuaded him that this woman of such refined tastes was likely to fall in love with him through the mail. But such a conquest could not have been his sole object. His expressed hope that the lady might bring Lord Selkirk to lobby against the war has a convincing ring, since we know that Jones had a greatly inflated idea of the Earl's political importance. To this extent the captain was writing as a military leader. Beyond this, however, Jones's best biographer, Samuel Eliot Morison, suggests that the hero harbored dreams of settling down as a Scottish landsman after the Revolution; with his letter he meant to inspire amity in his future neighbors!

This suggestion is a plausible explanation for the most "intimate" passage, in which Jones assumes a confessional tone and tells the Countess indirectly that he has no particular desire to live in America and that he is no stranger to the life of landed gentry.

Tho' I have drawn my Sword in the present generous Struggle for the rights of Men; yet I am not in Arms as an American, nor am I in pursuit of Riches. My Fortune is liberal enough, having no Wife nor Family, and having lived long enough to know that Riches cannot ensure Happiness. I profess myself a Citizen of the World, totally unfettered by the little mean distinctions of Climate or of Country, which diminish the benevolence of the Heart and set bounds to Philanthropy.

Before this War began I had at an early time of life, withdrawn from the Sea service, in favor of 'calm contemplation and Poetic ease.'

Captain Jones was never to find this life of rural bliss in Scotland, nor anywhere else; but in 1778 it seems to have been a real and enticing possibility in his mind.

Whatever else in the letter may have been devious, Jones's promise to restore the Selkirk silver was not. After more than five years of painstaking negotiation and personal expense, Jones got the plundered plate, which was worth about six hundred dollars, shipped back to the Selkirks in 1784. The breakfast tea leaves, we are assured, were still in the teapot.

NATIONAL GALLERIES OF SCOTLAND

Jean Antoine Houdon's 1780 bust of Jones was thought a good likeness.

was of the buffalo around me and the danger of being overwhelmed by them if my pony could not keep up the race. The new terror was a large prairie dog village, extending for half a mile or more up the valley. As the herd dashed into it, some of the animals stepped into the deep burrows, and near where I was riding I saw quite a number come to earth and now and then a comrade from behind fall over them. My trained buffalo horse here showed his wonderful sagacity. While running at full speed along with the herd, he kept his head down, and whenever a dangerous dog hole was in his path, he either stepped short or leaped over it and thus brought me through this new danger in safety. The race had now been kept up for several miles, and my carbine ammunition was nearly exhausted; while my pony, after his long day's work and rapid run, showed unmistakable signs of fatigue. My only hope was that he could hold out until we reached rougher ground, where the herd might divide. This came sooner than I expected.

As the valley narrowed, the side ravines came closer together at the bottom, and our course soon led us among them. The smaller gullies were leaped with ease by the buffalo close around me, and my pony held his own with the best of them. As the ravines became deeper, longer leaps were necessary, and my brave steed refused none of them. Soon the ravines became too wide for a single leap, and the buffalo plunged into them and scrambled up the opposite bank. My pony did the same, and several times I could have touched with my extended hands the buffalo on either side of me as we clambered together up the yielding sides of the narrow canyons we were crossing. This was hard work for all, and the buffalo showed the greater signs of fatigue, but no intentions of stopping in their mad career, except those that were disabled and went down in the fierce struggle to keep out of the way of those behind them.

As the valley narrowed, I saw ahead, perhaps a mile distant, a low butte, a little to the left of the course we were taking. This gave me new courage, for if I could only reach it, it would afford shelter, as the herd must pass on either side of it. Drawing a revolver, I began to shoot at the nearest buffalo on my left, and this caused them to draw away as far as the others would let them, and when one went down, I gained so much ground. They were now really more afraid of me and my steed than we were of them, and for this reason did not charge, as a single wounded buffalo might have done. Continuing my shooting more rapidly as we approached the butte, I gradually swung to the left, and when we came to it, I pulled my pony sharp around behind it, and let the great herd pass on.

Dismounting, I saw why my pony had seemed so foot-heavy during the last mile. He was covered with dust, nearly exhausted, and with bleeding flanks, distended forelegs, and blazing nostrils, he stood there quivering and breathing heavily, while the buffalo were passing within a few feet. We could not move until the herd had gone by, and it was more than an hour before the last of them left us alone. . . .

The danger was now over, and the pangs of hunger reminded me of the supper I had promised to secure for my comrades. One of the last stragglers of the herd in the twilight was a young heifer, and a shot brought her to my feet. To draw my hunting knife and remove the tongue and hump steaks, sufficient for our small party, was the work of a few minutes; and thus laden, I was ready to start for camp, some half a dozen miles to the eastward.

Meanwhile, I had not forgotten my . . . Indian pony. He had saved my life, and I did all I could for him. I took off his saddle, and I offered him the scanty contents of my pocket flask, but this he declined, although needing it more than myself. I started to lead him slowly in the direction of camp, but he soon made me understand that he was himself again, and after mounting, I gave him his head, and he hurried on in the darkness to where he knew our comrades were waiting for us. It was late as we approached camp, and the signal guns to guide us had for some time been flashing in the distance. My first duty on arriving was again to my weary steed, and for once my striker was not permitted to relieve me. I sang Pawnee's praises around the campfire that night. . . .

Poor Pawnee! He deserved a better fate than overtook him in his first campaign the next year. Grazing at night, he was bitten on the nose by a large rattlesnake. When found in the morning, his head was fearfully swollen, and all the whisky in camp could not save him. He was buried with military honors, and a double salute fired over his remains. If, in the happy hunting ground above, Pawnee does not have a place of honor, I shall lose all faith in the belief of the untutored Indian, who thinks—

admitted to that equal sky,
His faithful dog shall bear him company.

Mr. Penick is an associate professor of history at Loyola University in Chicago. He encountered Marsh's uncompleted autobiography, of which this article is a fragment, in the O. C. Marsh Papers at the Yale University Library. The excerpt appears here with the library's kind permission.

shocked despair. In this awful crisis of the young church only one Mormon responded with what must have amounted to joy: James Jesse Strang.

At the moment when a rifle ball struck Smith, causing him to fall to his death out of the second-story window of the Carthage jail, Strang was taking a solitary walk through the countryside outside Burlington. As the Prophet's life was extinguished, Strang said later, he heard celestial music, looked into the sky, and saw an angel accompanied by a heavenly host glide down onto the meadow in which he stood. The angel stretched forth a hand, anointing his head with oil as a sign that henceforth Prophet Strang was to be the supreme ruler of the Saints on earth.

For several days he did nothing. Perhaps he was looking for another sign. He certainly received one in the mail twelve days later. In an envelope postmarked "Nauvoo, June 19th," Strang received a letter supposedly written by Joseph Smith nine days before his assassination. In it Smith admitted to having wondered if Strang was under the influence of an evil spirit; but in the midst of his doubts, he wrote, God suddenly whirled him into the upper air. The moon and stars went out, the earth dissolved, and with heavenly music all about him Smith heard God reveal the Prophet's approaching martyrdom. Still aloft, Smith then heard God say, according to the letter, "And now behold my servant james j. Strang hath come to thee from far . . . & to him shall the gathering of the people be for he shall plant a stake of Zion in Wisconsin & I will establish it & there shall my people have peace & rest & shall not be mooved . . . & the name of the city shall be called voree which is being interpreted garden of peace . . . and now I command my servants the apostles & priests & elders of the church of the saints that they communicate & proclaim this my word to all the saints of God in all the world that they may be gathered unto and round about the city of Voree. . . ."

Within a month of the death of Joseph Smith, Strang was in Nauvoo, mounting a campaign to succeed him. At first he said nothing of the angel; he based his claim solely on the letter. But at once there were questions as to its authenticity. Ironically, most were directed to the postmark, which is valid, instead of to the signature, which an expert in 1950 described as a manifest forgery. It was soon clear that more than a questionable letter would be needed if Strang, a relatively recent convert, was going to outdistance such stalwart contestants as the Wild Ram of the Mountains, Lyman Wight; the Archer of Paradise, Parley P. Pratt; or the most formidable of them all, the Lion of the Lord, Brigham Young. All these men enjoyed the prestige of being among Smith's twelve apostles at the time of his assassination. They were known and respected not only in Nauvoo but wherever there were Mormons.

But James Jesse Strang had one incalculable advantage over all of them, and particularly over his chief rival, the stolid Brigham Young. The Mormon Church had been founded by a prophet, a soothsaying, crystal-gazing seer who soared with the angelic host and talked to God Himself. To those who felt that Smith's successor as head of the Church of Latter-day Saints should also be a prophet, Strang was a good choice. Three of the twelve apostles supported Strang, as did Joseph Smith's mother and his brother William. And scores of other Mormons suddenly found that the words of a familiar Mormon hymn, number 297—"A church without a Prophet, Is not the Church for me;/It has no head to guide it; In it I would not be"—had new meaning. They migrated from Nauvoo to Strang's new Mormon "stake" at Voree, outside Burlington. Brigham Young was not given to revelations, but he did go so far as to ban the singing of that hymn.

But a full-fledged prophet in the Joseph Smith tradition must have a testament. It had come to Smith in the form of *The Book of Mormon;* Strang was to receive it in *The Book of the Law of the Lord.* In each instance, an angel conducted the prophet to buried plates on which the holy writ was inscribed in a foreign language. Strang received the first angelic alert of the impending discovery early in 1845. That fall the angel appeared again and showed Strang the precise spot at which to dig. He led four of his disciples to the spot, then stood apart as they commenced to dig. After digging, then chopping their way through the roots of an oak tree, then using pick-axes to penetrate a layer of rock, they finally came to three brass plates.

Eighteen years earlier, when Joseph Smith had dug up his buried plates in upstate New York, he had allowed no one to see them. When anyone was in their presence, Smith kept the plates covered with a handkerchief. Strang showed his to his awed followers, then went into seclusion for a week to translate their strange markings, which he later reported to be passages in certain "lost Levantine languages."

The Brighamites charged that Strang's plates had been fashioned from an old brass kettle and that the inscriptions on them were unintelligible "hen tracks." Strang insisted that they were the record left by Rajah Manchore of Vorito, an Oriental potentate who millenniums ago on the site of the Wisconsin frontier had ruled

78

a godlike people, now levelled to dust but destined one day to rise again. The instrument of their resurrection was to be the divinely guided prophet who would discover and translate the constitution of their theocratic monarchy. As the rajah inscribed it on the plates: "The forerunner men shall kill, but a mighty prophet there shall dwell. I will be his strength, and he shall bring forth my records." The forerunner was the slain Joseph; the prophet was his successor, James. It is regrettable that this is the rajah's sole appearance in history, for the spectacle of this exotic figure transplanted to the Northwest Territory has the same incongruous charm as the appearance (courtesy of Mark Twain) about the same time of the "disappeared Dauphin, Looy the Seventeen" on a raft carrying a runaway boy and an escaped slave down the Mississippi.

From 1845 to 1848 Strang waged a vigorous campaign to succeed Joseph Smith as leader of the Church of Latter-day Saints. He travelled to all the big cities of the eastern seaboard, preaching and debating. He published a newspaper and wrote news stories, editorials, and reports of his travels. He repeatedly denounced Brigham Young as an imposter and finally "excommunicated" him, delivering him over to "the buffetings of Satan." He assembled his own twelve apostles and created the Primitive Church of Latter-day Saints, with himself as leader and prophet. And he proceeded to develop his utopian Mormon community, Voree, in southwestern Wisconsin.

Strang's strengths and weaknesses as a leader are vividly revealed in his efforts to build his own church organization and the theocratic community that it would serve. To seize control of the Mormon Church, Strang needed even more than divine documentation of his legitimacy as Joseph Smith's successor. He needed a cadre of experienced Mormons to represent his cause not only in Nauvoo but in the great population centers of the East that were the recruiting grounds for the church: Baltimore, Washington, Philadelphia, and New York. Lacking time to train men for this role, Strang assembled the leadership for his church from among those who had defected from Smith and Young. Some of them had good credentials, but many were scoundrels. A superb example of the latter was George J. Adams.

Adams was an actor and a preacher, noted for his taste for crude bombast, loose women, and bourbon. A tall, striking man, he had played the heavy in such melodramas as *The Idiot Witness* and *Pizaro, or the Death of Rolla* in a Mormon repertory company at Nauvoo. But when his womanizing came to Brigham Young's attention, Adams was thrown out of the church for "under the sacred garb of religion . . . practising the most disgraceful and diabolical conduct." Packing up his theatrical costumes, Adams drifted to Ohio, where he came to Strang's attention.

Strang was somewhat cautious in recruiting Adams. When questioned about his having been thrown out of the Mormon Church, Adams replied in writing that he was a victim of "base phalshoods," including the charges that he was a drunkard and a fornicator; the truth was, according to Adams, that Young and his apostles were deeply jealous of Adams' ability to spellbind his listeners "whereaver and whenever I lift up my voice." Adams confessed to having some doubts about Strang, but he resolved these by conferring with God, who "condescended in a glorious manner" to verify that Strang was, indeed, the true prophet.

Adams reached Voree in the spring of 1846. With him was another prominent Mormon who had fallen out with the leaders at Nauvoo: Dr. John C. Bennett— former major general of the Mormon Legion (the Latter-day Saints' armed force) and also Nauvoo's leading abortionist. While his medical skills had been in great demand in a community where plural marriage was already widely if secretly practiced, Bennet had made the mistake of becoming nonclinically interested in a nineteen-year-old girl named Nancy Rigdon, to whom Joseph Smith had taken a particular liking. Bennett was excommunicated in 1842 and like Adams eventually decided to throw in his lot with Strang.

Voree, when Adams and Bennett got there, was an unpromising frontier settlement of little more than a thousand people living in log houses and tents. The prospect of settling in this rude village must have been unexciting indeed—and not merely because of its size. In Nauvoo, then the largest city in Illinois, Joseph Smith's paramonarchical state had engulfed the community. It organized the theatres, the army, businesses, schools, newspapers, and the government itself. The church, it seemed, was merely another sphere it controlled.

Bennett proposed to Strang, in effect, the re-creation of a Nauvoo at Voree. Specifically, he suggested that Strang lay the basis for such a community by devising a secret order that would govern the Strangite kingdom of God on earth. The order would be organized along feudal lines, with noblemen, viceroys, grand councillors, and, above them all, God's earthly regent, the king himself, James Jesse Strang. To the man who at nineteen had secretly sworn to rival Caesar and Napoleon and had spent a day try-

Strang's fourth wife, Sarah Wright

ing to contrive a scheme to marry into the House of Hanover, Bennett's suggestion had the sound of Destiny.

The Halcyon Order of the Illuminati bears abundant evidence of the blending of the powerful monarchical leanings of Strang with the brilliant charlatanism of Bennett. An initiate into the order, with ranks of chevaliers, earls, marshals, and cardinals drawn up around him in a darkened room, took an oath to

uphold sustain and obey the said James J. Strang and his lawful successors, if any he has, each in his time as the Imperial primate and actual sovereign Lord and King on Earth and as my true and lawful Sovereign wheresoever and in whatsoever kingdom state or dominion I may be; and in preference to the laws, commandments and persons of any other Kings, Potentates, or States whatsoever. . . .

Upon swearing to the oath, the initiate into the Illuminati knelt before the king, who anointed his head with oil. And miraculously, according to the testimony of more than one member of the order, the initiate's head would thereupon radiate with a glowing halo. Even given his deep yearning for power—kingly power—it is remarkable enough that James Strang finally would find himself on a throne. But it is perhaps even more remarkable that on their knees before that throne were rugged American pioneers imperturbably forfeiting both their souls and their American citizenship.

But before the top nobility of the order had been initiated, the summer of 1846 had arrived and Strang had gone East on business. The blueprint of the kingdom of God on earth had been sketched out; now the prophet needed to round up the Saints and march them to Voree. Accompanied by Bennett, Adams, and some of his other apostles, Strang began in earnest to woo the Mormon Church of the martyred Joseph Smith. Brigham Young's followers had already started their long trek from Nauvoo to the West when James Jesse Strang headed for Ohio. His objective: to capture the first Mormon Church established by Smith, the Kirtland Stake.

When Strang appeared in Kirtland, he was no mere upstart. He had three of Joseph Smith's twelve apostles in his Primitive Church of Latter-day Saints. He had the support of Smith's mother and brother William. Moreover, the Brighamites were in disarray as they fled westward from the ruins of Nauvoo. As he rose to speak to the Kirtland Saints assembled for their morning worship one Sunday in the summer of 1846, James Jesse Strang must have realized that this could be a decisive day in his life. Even though he was small and thoroughly unprepossessing in appearance, Strang could galvanize an audience. On that Sunday he preached for eight hours in what one of his followers described as his "most rapid manner." It was a superb performance. The Kirtland Saints were dazzled and won over. The new prophet

took possession of the first Mormon temple; then with George J. Adams and others, he headed for Philadelphia, New York, and Boston with the plan of setting the Mormon churches there "in order," that is, winning them over from the Brighamite faction to the Strangite.

Although Kirtland was the most heartening victory that summer, Strang made many converts throughout the East. His attack was two-pronged. First, he denounced Brigham Young and his apostles for teaching that "polygamy, fornication, and adultery are required by the command of God in the upbuilding of his kingdom." He climaxed his denunciation of them with what must be one of the most revolting curses·uttered by a nineteenth-century clergyman: "may their bones rot in the living tomb of their flesh; may their flesh generate from its own corruptions a loathsome life for others; may their blood swarm with a leprous life of motelike, ghastly corruption feeding on flowing life, generating chilling agues and burning fevers. May peace and home be names forgotten to them; and the beauty they have betrayed to infamy, may it be to their eyes a crawling mass of putridity and battening corruption. . . ."

The second prong of Strang's attack was an appeal to his listeners to gather into the fold at Voree planned for them by God and revealed by God to his two prophets, Joseph and James. That fall and winter Voree harvested the fruits of the prophet's eastern swing, and the village nearly doubled in size. But it was also gathering the bitter harvest of Bennett's secret Order of the Illuminati. Somehow the covenant of the order leaked out and by January, 1847, two thousand copies had been printed along with a handbill denouncing it as an undemocratic cabal whose members were banded together for purposes of iniquity. Perhaps the handbill's most telling thrust was at the initiation ceremony. It did not deny that the heads of the initiates glowed, but pointed out that this was a hoax engineered by Strang, who rubbed their heads with a mixture of olive oil and phosphorus. One apostate even found the bottle and repeated the "miracle."

The attack on the Illuminati was only the first of a series of harassments by local non-Mormons, or "Gentiles," as the Latter-day Saints dubbed everyone else. As Strang's converts made their way toward Voree from the East, it became a common Gentile practice to stop their wagons a few miles outside of town and try to convince them they had made a terrible mistake. Shrewd Gentile farmers also curbed the growth of the community by early buying up much of the land in and around it and offering it for sale to the Saints at prohibitive prices.

In spite of his blunders in the selection of some of his lieutenants, Strang was capable of decisive leadership. By the winter of 1846–47 he saw that Voree was doomed and that a new site needed to be found that possessed an abundance of fertile land and isolation from hostile Gentiles. And he had a prophetic hunch that he had seen the New Jerusalem from the deck of a Great Lakes steamer on his way from Buffalo to Chicago. After moving through the Straits of Mackinac, the steamer had passed among some lush, green islands fifty miles southwest of the straits. It occurred to Strang at the time that these islands would offer the land as well as the safety that his kingdom needed. The events of the following winter greatly increased the appeal of those remote islands. Soon the garden of peace reverberated with the rumble of excommunications. William Smith, Joseph's brother, was charged with being one of the most lascivious libertines ever to prey upon American womanhood and was consigned to the buffetings of Satan. His lengthy defense contains little of interest except for one minor point: he claimed to have discovered the bottle of olive oil and phosphorus used at initiations.

John C. Bennett, general and prime minister, whose talent for mischief was not small, was also excommunicated and departed the scene with hardly a flurry. When he had broken with Joseph Smith he had written a series of scurrilous newspaper articles denouncing his former friends. This time he quietly drifted off to New England to raise chickens. Of Strang's more flamboyant lieutenants, only Councillor Adams stayed on. The Brighamites ridiculed him for pursuing a twin career as actor and preacher, but the prophet tolerated not only Adams' acting but his drinking and lechery, in return for notable services on behalf of the Strangite kingdom. Strang even defended Adams by asking the Saints, "Isn't it true that no less a man than David danced naked before the daughters of Israel?"

In the spring of 1847 Strang and four Mormons from Voree visited the islands Strang had seen the previous summer. The largest of the group of a dozen, Big Beaver, is thirteen miles long and six wide. It has broad white sand beaches the length of its eastern shore and sand dunes and bluffs along its western side. At the northern end is one of the finest sheltered harbors in the Great Lakes. The island is in the midst of what was in mid-nineteenth century—and remained until the advent of the sea lamprey—one of the best fishing areas in the lakes. The land was fertile and well timbered. It was an ideal spot for a utopian community.

At the appropriate time, Strang announced that he had been visited by an angel who instructed him to move his colony to "a land amid wide waters and covered with large timber, with a deep broad bay on one side of it." Clearly this was Beaver Island; and evidently the angel knew that Indian claims had already been invalidated and that shortly the federal government would open Beaver and the surrounding islands for settlement. From

1848 on, the Mormons streamed from Voree to Beaver. They found the islands practically a virgin wilderness, and with industry, intelligence, and dedication they named the rivers, lakes, bays, and hills of Beaver Island with proper Biblical names; they cleared the fields and planted them, laid out a network of roads, and erected sturdy log houses. The church, the jail, the royal press, and the king's residence were clustered along the shores of the fine harbor in a settlement they immodestly called St. James—the name it bears today. In fact, in many important ways the island has changed very little. It has approximately the same population as in Strang's heyday: two thousand; the main road is called the King's Highway; the highest sand dune is Mount Pisgah; the large inland lake at the south end is Lake Genesereth; the chief river is the Jordan; the shallow baptismal lake at the north end is Font Lake; and the splendid harbor, Paradise Bay.

Brigham Young found his New Jerusalem at the end of a two-thousand-mile trail, and as the world capital of Mormonism, Salt Lake City has since then prospered and multiplied despite its remoteness. James's kingdom was far more accessible to the Mormon recruiting areas of the East and Midwest; yet it was equally isolated from the Gentile world, richly blessed with fertile fields, virgin forests, and superb fishing grounds; and it is as inviting now as it was a century ago. But today it contains not a single Saint.

What was fatal to Strang and his kingdom was the alliance between his disaffected followers—few as they were—and the hostile Gentiles who, even in northern Michigan, saw this tiny colony as a threat to the Republic, to orthodox Christianity, to conventional sexual morality, and to economic privilege—specifically, the right to use the island as a base for fishing operations and trading with the Indians.

Although the few Gentiles who occupied Beaver Island when the Saints began arriving were unfriendly, they were quickly outnumbered and outmaneuvered by Strang and his followers. Their unfriendliness hardened into resentment as they observed the Mormons rename the lakes, rivers, and hills on the island and treat them as their God-given inheritance. The Gentile trading post stood on Whisky Point, a hooklike projection of land that protected the harbor. It was aptly named, for a major part of Gentile business consisted of bartering whisky for fish caught by the Indians. The ultimate source of Gentile hostility to Strang, however, was not on Whisky Point but on Mackinac, the small island at the tip of Michigan's lower peninsula. A century earlier it had been the center of the fur trade for almost half the North American continent; then for a while it had served as a fuelling station for wood-burning steamers. With the fur trade a trickle of what it had been and the island's timber all chopped down, Mackinac in the mid-nineteenth century existed largely on its past reputation as a trading center.

Strang was quick to perceive this. His paper, "Some Remarks on the Natural History of Beaver Islands, Michigan," was published in the Smithsonian Institution's Annual Report, 1854, and remained the definitive work for nearly a century. As a student of the island's economy, he traced the barrels of whisky from the warehouses at Mackinac to the trading post at Whisky Point, where they were used to produce what was called Indian whisky: two gallons of common whisky or unrectified spirits were dumped into thirty gallons of water; red pepper was added to give it fire, tobacco to make it more intoxicating. For thirty years, Strang reported, the fish shipped from the rich grounds around Beaver Island had been paid for in large part with Indian whisky. It cost five cents a gallon to make and was sold to the Indians for fifty cents a gallon by the cask, twenty-five cents for a quart, or six cents for a drink. The boats that brought the whisky returned to Mackinac laden with fish.

Strang exposed this illegal exploitation of the Indians in numerous articles in his newspaper *The Northern Islander* and in a forty-eight page pamphlet, "Ancient and Modern Michilimackinac, Including an Account of the Controversy between Mackinac and the Mormons." Even though there were only twenty or thirty Indian families on Beaver, their presence made the island more attractive to Strang and his followers, who shared Joseph Smith's notion that the Indians were members of a fallen race, the Lamanites, mentioned in *The Book of Mormon.* Proselyting among this "noble and intellectual race of men," to use Strang's words, had been one reason for choosing Beaver Island.

Fishing rights and trade with the Indians may have been the two basic causes of friction between Gentiles and Saints, but in terms of interest, especially in newspapers in Michigan and throughout the East, these were eclipsed by something far more sensational: polygamy.

By this time the widespread practice of "spiritual wifery" among the top leadership of Brigham Young's Mormons had become common knowledge. This made it an ideal issue by which the Strangites could differentiate their sect from the Brighamites. In 1847 one of the elders of Strang's church, John E. Page, had issued a statement denouncing polygamy in which he declared: "We have talked hours, yea, even days with President Strang, and we find to our utmost satisfaction that he does not believe in or cherish the doctrine of polygamy in any manner, shape, or form imaginable whatever."

The following spring, when the migration to Beaver Island was under way, Strang held a conference at which members of the Strangite sect living outside Voree assembled to meet the prophet and discuss the future of the church. One of those who attended was a seventeen-year-old schoolteacher from Charlotte, Michigan, whose parents had switched from the Brighamite to the Strangite church. Elvira Eliza Smith was bright, modest, devout, and attractive. She deeply impressed Prophet Strang. She returned to Michigan, and some months later she was visited by an emissary from the prophet, Councillor Adams, who bore a remarkable proposal.

He told Elvira that the prophet had received from God, by means of an angel, the divine plan for the kingdom of God on earth. James Jesse Strang was to rule the kingdom as king and vice-regent of God. *And* the new society was to be polygamous: the king was to set the example for his subjects! Then Adams, the histrionic old lecher, with suitable dramatic flourishes, hand-pressings, and other business, came to the point: Would Elvira accept the honor of being the king's first plural wife and a queen of his kingdom? That Elvira quickly accepted tells us something about Councillor Adams' special talents and a great deal about the prophet's remarkable ability to convince his followers of his divine mission.

On July 13, 1849, in defiance of the laws of Michigan, the United States, and—up till then—the Primitive Church of Latter-day Saints, James and Elvira were "married" in a bedchamber somewhere in Michigan. As a lawyer, Strang knew their marriage was legally impossible; and as one of the loudest opponents of Mormon polygamy, he recognized that in terms of the struggle for power within the Mormon Church, it was politically dangerous. So he cropped his young bride's dark hair, bought her a black broadcloth suit and a black silk hat like his, gave her the name Charles J. Douglass, and took her with him as his nephew and secretary on his customary fall and winter recruiting drive through the major cities of the eastern seaboard. While his first wife, Mary, and their four children stayed with his relatives in Chautauqua County, New York, the prophet and his bride honeymooned in New York City. In letters to Mary, Strang wrote of "Charley's" being with him, but we do not know whether Mary was hoodwinked by the fiction of this newly discovered nephew. At any rate, there were those who were not.

That October, during a church meeting in New York City over which Strang was presiding, with Charley beside him as secretary, the newlyweds had a jolting experience. After Strang concluded his sermon and pronounced the benediction, one of his apostles jumped to his feet to accuse Strang of "adultery, fornication, and spiritual wifery."

It is a delightful irony that the only report we have of this contretemps is to be found in Strang's newspaper *The Gospel Herald* in a lengthy article signed "C. J. Douglass." Elvira, alias Charley, describes how President

Strang preached "with burning and matchless eloquence, in words that seemed to fall from angels' lips." While he spoke, Apostle Lorenzo D. Hickey listened with "a kind of nervous twitching which sometimes marks incipient insanity"; then, the sermon over, he jumped up and shouted his accusation at Strang. The account ends with the comment that Strang's refutation of the charges against him "convinced every person present that Hickey's accusations were all utterly false." The same issue of *The Gospel Herald*, November 22, 1849, contains the report by the phrenologist who found Strang lacking in "tact and cunning."

As spring approached, the thirty-seven-year-old prophet faced the necessity of returning to Beaver Island with his new bride, his first wife, and their four children. But his supply of tact and cunning was so large that Strang was able to make the shift from monogamy to polygamy without in the least rippling the waters of Paradise Bay. He matter-of-factly announced that he had just translated one passage of 165 characters on the sacred plates the angel had led him to in Wisconsin. It read: "Thou shalt not take unto thee a multitude of wives disproportioned to thy inheritance, and thy substance; nor shalt thou take wives to vex those thou hast; neither shalt thou put away one to take another." This was a bit subtle, but the implication was clear: with proper reservations, a Saint could have several wives.

At the same time the prophet finally disclosed to his people that in obedience to Chapter XX of the *Book of the Law of the Lord* he would shortly be crowned king. The *Book* said: "God has chosen his servant James to be King; He hath made him his Apostle to all nations; He hath established Him a prophet above the Kings of the Earth; and appointed him King in Zion; by His voice did he call Him, and He sent his angels unto him to ordain him." Despite some wavering on the question of whether the pronouns describing himself should be capitalized, Strang had a feeling for Biblical language that Joseph Smith lacked. Mark Twain said of Smith that "Whenever he found his speech growing too modern—which was about every sentence or two—he ladled in a few such Scriptural phrases as 'exceeding sore,' 'and it came to pass,' etc., and made things satisfactory again." Strang had more the hang of it.

The coronation occurred on July 8, 1850 (Elvira's twentieth birthday), in the log tabernacle, a roofless structure eighty feet long. A fifteen-year-old girl who

Harper's Monthly, MARCH 1882

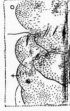

Only Strang was able to translate the symbols on the brass plates he "found" in Wisconsin authorizing his kingdom.

managed to squeeze into the tabernacle later wrote an awed account of the ceremony. A trumpet sounded, and James Strang was escorted into the tabernacle by the council and the twelve apostles, followed by the quorums, or minor orders of the ministry. The king wore a long flowing robe of bright red. The procession moved the length of the tabernacle to the platform on which the coronation would take place. Awaiting them there, garbed in the most regal costume he could assemble from his collection, was the actor-preacher president of the council, George J. Adams. He towered over the little bearded king enveloped in his red robe. The climax of the ceremony came when Adams, wearing a short tin sword attached to a brass-studded belt, with enormous dignity held out the crown in both hands. It was a shiny metal ring with a cluster of glass stars in the front. The July sun shone into the roofless tabernacle and made the stars sparkle as Adams slowly lowered the crown onto the elongated and perspiring head of King James Jesse Strang.

For the next few years this ceremony did not seem as pathetically absurd as it does today. The island's economy flourished. The Chicago-Buffalo steamer made sixty stops a year at St. James, and many other vessels sailed into Paradise Bay for fish, firewood, and lumber. In Mackinac the reign of King Jimmy was no longer a subject for crude jokes. The king's handling of the island's polity was too impressive: he combined with remarkable adroitness the throne and the ballot box.

Strang ruled the Saints with the absolute power of a divinely ordained monarch; but at the same time he ran as a Democrat for the Michigan state legislature and won two terms. He introduced a bill to have the Beaver Islands incorporated into a new county; and when this passed he controlled that county and another on the mainland that had a bloc of Mormon voters.

By 1855 King Strang was at the peak of his power. His kingdom embraced Beaver Island and certain outlying islands with a total population of about twenty-six hundred Saints. His people were prosperous and, for the most part, loyal and happy. And the king's household had waxed most royally. In 1852 he had married Betsy McNutt, a thirty-one-year-old maiden, and she, like Mary his first wife, and Elvira his second, bore him four children. Then in the summer and fall of 1855, he married two teen-age cousins, Sarah and Phoebe Wright, each of whom shortly became pregnant. The king and his four wives and children lived in a sturdy but trim log house overlooking Paradise Bay. (Mary, his first wife, had taken her children and moved back to Wisconsin, evidently feeling that six was a crowd.) Sarah wrote of their life together, "[We] had separate rooms [but] . . . all met in prayer and ate at the same table." Of Strang she said, "He was a very mild-spoken, kind man to his family, although his word was law—we were all honest in our religion and made things as pleasant as possible."

Through hard work, shrewdness, and what would today be called charisma, James Strang had, unbelievably, fulfilled the outlandish dreams of royal power that he had confided to his diary as a frustrated farm boy of nineteen. But if the ascent to power had been slow and uncertain, the descent was to be breathtakingly swift.

Beneath the seemingly tranquil surface of life on Beaver Island there were some fairly powerful currents of dissension. How deep these ran it is difficult to say, for this was a totalitarian society in which expressions of dissent were dealt with harshly. Marriage with Gentiles was forbidden; drinking tea, coffee, or alcohol was outlawed; the use of tobacco was forbidden; pantalets under skirts were required by law, and women who broke the law exposed their husbands to punishment. Even men's clothing was regulated by law. And the punishments were of Old Testament severity, meted out with a lash made of beech switches toughened by heating and twisting. For example, for "lying, tale-bearing, and endeavoring to incite to mischief," the culprit was stripped to the waist and lashed thirty-nine strokes.

King Strang's harsh, autocratic rule and the deep enmity it engendered among some of the islanders would probably have been insufficient by itself to topple his kingdom. But Gentile antagonism on both the island and the mainland had been building against the Mormons from their first appearance on Beaver in 1847. As the Saints had grown in economic and political power, the number of incidents between them and the Gentiles had increased in frequency and gravity. The introduction of polygamy and the formal establishment of the kingdom had exacerbated Gentile feelings of hostility that were already nearly unbearable.

It did not help matters at all that the newspapers, particularly the Detroit *Free Press* and Detroit *Advertiser and Tribune*, found King Strang irresistible. They printed lurid—and largely false—accounts of Mormon sexual license, thievery, and political chicanery. Councillor George J. Adams, a few years after Strang's coronation, incurred the royal wrath by bringing a prostitute over from the mainland and passing her off as his wife: he was thrown out. He then spread stories, which the Detroit papers eagerly broadcast, of assassinations and torture and of a huge Mormon counterfeit mill operating in

a cave in Mount Pisgah. During the spring of 1851 President Millard Fillmore, visiting his brother in Detroit, read of scandalous events on Beaver Island and decided to take action. He placed the U.S.S. *Michigan*, the first ironclad vessel built for the U.S. Navy, at the disposal of the U. S. District Attorney, George C. Bates.

Due process was observed by having the governor of Michigan request federal intervention. Then, armed with warrants charging Strang and most of his top officials with treason, counterfeiting, trespass, theft, and several other crimes—oddly enough, not including polygamy—the district attorney, accompanied by a marshal and a judge, sailed into Paradise Bay on the *Michigan* one night in May, 1851. The attorney, leading a body of sailors each armed with a Navy revolver and cutlass, proceeded stealthily toward Strang's house, their way lit by a covered ship's lantern. After stationing a boatswain at each end of the house, District Attorney Bates crept up the stairs until he found himself in "a long, low room, where wide berths, heavily draped with stunning calico, shielded beds like the berths and staterooms of steamers, which proved to be occupied by Mormon women four in a bed."

The account of the raid on the seraglio by the intrepid D.A. appears to be mostly romantic nonsense. At no time did the king's palace have a harem. And with Mary in Wisconsin, Strang in the summer of 1851 was living with the only other wife he had at the time, Elvira. When Strang was awakened, he coolly examined the warrants and shortly thereafter peaceably surrendered himself and thirty-one of his disciples. They were transported to Detroit on the *Michigan*, and Strang pleaded the defendants' case before a jury of ten Whigs and two Democrats. In his closing statement to the jury, Strang, the lawyer turned preacher, made an eloquent speech in which he drew analogies between himself and Jesus. This had been the basis of his defense throughout the trial: that he and his followers were victims of religious persecution—as they indeed were. The jury agreed and acquitted them all.

Following the trial there were numerous instances of Mormon-Gentile friction, but none compared in violence to "the Battle of Pine River" in the summer of 1853. The trouble started when Strang tried to use his considerable police power in Manitou and Emmett counties to halt the sale of Indian whisky to the Indians in the vicinity of Pine River on the mainland—present-day Charlevoix. Pine River fishermen regarded Strang as an ungodly polygamist and a power-mad dictator who was trying to expand his empire.

On July 12, 1853, the Mormon sheriff of Emmett County, together with thirteen other Beaver Islanders, put in at Pine River on a peaceful mission: to issue calls for jury duty in the circuit court at St. James the following week. As they were leaving in two boats, the Pine River settlers opened fire on them from close range on the beach. The Mormons, six of them wounded, hastily pulled out of range; but before they had well started on their twenty-five-mile trip across open water to Beaver Island, they saw that they were being pursued by three boatloads of Pine River fishermen. For ten miles the chase continued, the Mormons managing to stay just beyond range of gunfire; then the fishermen began to close the gap, and bullets started striking the Mormon boats again. Incredibly, at this moment a Buffalo-Chicago steamer came along, and the captain took the exhausted and bleeding oarsmen aboard. The furious fishermen, helpless against the large vessel, turned around and headed back for Pine River.

Strang called the survival of the Mormons "an extraordinary instance of the care of God for his creatures." He declared in an extra of his newspaper *The Islander* that it would be satisfying to ravage the Pine River settlement, "but the moral effect of sending half a dozen to State Prison is worth more than the death of them all. Legal remedies are better than violent ones."

But for those to whom no legal remedies are available —or seem to be—violent ones sometimes have an irresistible appeal. In 1856 four such men, each of whom had suffered under Strang's harsh rule, plotted his assassination. Dr. Hezekiah McCulloch, a sometime physician who had held some of the highest offices in the Strangite church, had fallen into disgrace because of a vice that Strang detested, drunkenness; he was the chief conspirator. His accomplices were Thomas Bedford, who had once been severely whipped for adultery; Alexander Wentworth, a dandy who chafed under the king's repressive laws; and a "Doctor" Atkyn, an itinerant daguerreotypist, con man, and blackmailer whom Strang had threatened to boot off the island.

When McCulloch and Atkyn made a trip to the mainland to buy firearms and ammunition, Strang calmly reported in the next day's issue of *The Islander*, May 22, 1856: "Two doctors left here yesterday, and today two or three ignorant persons say they are on an errand of mischief." The king was even unperturbed when the conspirators came back, set up a target range, and practiced their marksmanship. By mid-June Strang's tone was stridently overconfident: "We laugh in bitter scorn at all these threats," he wrote in *The Islander*. What King Strang for all his political acumen had failed to learn was that no autocrat can afford to laugh at threats.

The conspirators timed their assault to coincide with the arrival of the *Michigan* at St. James; Dr. McCulloch had somehow persuaded the captain to bring the warship to Beaver again. On Monday, June 16, 1856, it put in at the dock in front of a store run by McCulloch, and the captain sent his pilot to summon King Strang. Why we do not know; but it is entirely possible the captain was a party to the plot. It was 7 P.M. and the prophet and his four wives had just finished the evening meal, so Strang obligingly walked to the pier. As he approached it, Bedford and Wentworth stepped out of McCulloch's store and rapidly caught up with Strang from the rear. Wentworth aimed his revolver and shot Strang in the head at close range. As he fell, the prophet turned to face his assailants, and Wentworth shot him in the face below the right eye. This caused Strang to roll over, and as he did so Bedford fired his pistol into the prophet's back. After pistol-whipping the severely wounded Strang about the face and head, Bedford and Wentworth ran up the gangplank of the *Michigan* and asked for—and got— protection. Strang was carried to a nearby house, where the *Michigan*'s surgeon examined him and bandaged his wounds, but it was probably obvious to him that Strang was mortally wounded.

The leading Saints hastily conferred in the printing office, and Sheriff Joshua Miller wrote a note to Captain McBlair of the *Michigan* requesting that he join the sheriff and others there to discuss what to do with Bedford and Wentworth. The captain refused.

When the iron ship sailed out of Paradise Bay at ten o'clock the following morning, Bedford, Wentworth, and McCulloch were aboard. The captain said he would turn them over to the sheriff at Mackinac. He did—and, not surprisingly, within five minutes the three conspirators were at liberty and being feted as heroes by the townspeople. Beaver Island's threat to Mackinac had finally been destroyed.

Twelve years earlier, when Joseph Smith was assassinated, the Mormon Church had suffered a similar crisis, but a half dozen leaders defied the Gentile mobs and reassembled the Saints. James Strang was in an even better position than Smith had been to bring this about, for he did not die for over three weeks after being shot, and he was fully conscious most of that time. But when his confused, leaderless followers sought his advice, the dying king merely said that each man should take care of his family. When they pressed him to appoint a successor, he said, "I do not want to talk about it."

The collapse of the kingdom was not at first apparent to the Gentiles, who had been given more than one painful lesson on Mormon durability. Ten days after the shooting, the *Michigan*, with the three conspirators aboard, sailed into Paradise Bay, and there was talk of arresting Mormons. But when a large number of Strang's people assembled, the vessel steamed off to Mackinac. This was enough, however, to convince the Saints that their king would have to be taken to a safer place. On June 28 he was carried by steamer to Wisconsin.

But nothing filled the vacuum left by the departed

king, and as this became increasingly clear to Gentile raiding parties from Mackinac, they became bolder. The climax was reached on July 5 when a mob, largely from Mackinac, arrived in a flotilla of boats to push the Mormons off Beaver Island. Bands of half-drunk, armed men roamed the island, driving Mormon farmers and their families at gunpoint to the dock at St. James, where steamers came to transport the dispossessed to Chicago and Detroit. One boat took 490 to Chicago; another took 300. They were forced to leave behind everything but their clothing: livestock, household goods, even their provisions. And, of course, their well-tended farms and orchards. The dispirited Mormons were so overwhelmed that none of them resisted to any extent. There was no gunfire. Yet within the span of a day or so, an entire community of approximately 2,600 men, women, and children was ruthlessly uprooted and cast out. One reputable Michigan historian, Byron M. Cutcheon, has called the fifth of July, 1856, "the most disgraceful day in Michigan history."

As King Strang lay dying in Voree, few of his subjects were with him. Two of his wives, Betsy and Phoebe, nursed him; only two apostles were at hand. On July 9, 1856, almost exactly six years after his coronation, the king died and was buried in Voree.

The kingdom had fallen with the king. And the Primitive Church of Latter-day Saints collapsed not long after the death of its sole prophet, James Jesse Strang. Had he appointed a strong successor, both kingdom and church would have had a chance to survive his death. But his failure to do so was completely in character.

Strang was a gifted man. But his very considerable personal magnetism, his powerful will, and his immense capacity for hope were not possessed primarily by a dream of service to God nor by a project of social reform. What possessed him was an adolescent boy's dream of royal power, a dream that focused monomaniacally on the crown itself. The thought of passing the crown on to someone else did not occur to him; and when it was suggested, it was a notion devoid of any appeal. "After me," King Strang must have thought, "—nothing."

A professor of English at the University of Michigan, Robert P. Weeks has a summer home on Beaver Island and has made research on the Strang settlement a vacation hobby. Among important printed sources, he recommends The Kingdom of Saint James, *by Milo M. Quaife (1930), and* Crown of Glory: The Life of James J. Strang, *by O. W. Riegel (1935)—both published by the Yale University Press.*

A Century of American Realism CONTINUED FROM PAGE 15

resentful of the crassness of American society, the exploitation of the poor, the brutality of American corporations. James became more and more struck by the corruption of society, in England and this country. His analysis took the form of sexual allegory—the attempt to get money through marriage, or the betrayal of adultery became symbols in his work of the corruption of society as a whole.

James was disillusioned with his society, but a good writer always is. The mood of anxiety and bitterness which many Americans feel right now certain American novelists felt as early as the 1920's—F. Scott Fitzgerald for instance. *The Great Gatsby* is one of the great American social novels. *The Great Gatsby, Tender Is the Night,* and the unfinished novel about Hollywood, *The Last Tycoon,* were all immensely prophetic documents as well as beautiful novels. Nowadays we teach them to undergraduates and say: "You see, that's American life." But in the 1920's one couldn't have said this so easily, though it was already true. In the 1890's Dreiser and Crane saw things that many a smug American wouldn't see for thirty or forty years.

How were novelists influenced by World War I?

The basic thing about the First World War and American novelists was that so many of them got into it. When relatively few Americans were actually in the Army, Hemingway, Faulkner, Fitzgerald, and many others were in the war. They found in the war a great sense of adventure. Hemingway was so eager to get into it that he enlisted as an ambulance volunteer. He was on the Italian front long before America entered the war. At the very beginning many writers felt this was their chance to get to Europe, to participate in things. All the wonderful works of fiction of the World War—Dos Passos' *1919,* Hemingway's *A Farewell to Arms,* even Faulkner's *Soldiers' Pay*—can be described conventionally as tales of disillusionment, but actually they are tales of adventure. These writers had a great sense of buoyant confidence; this was their moment. You can see in *1919* and in Hemingway's stories the great sense of freshness and adventure. They were free of American provincialism; they were free of their parents. (Many were still young enough to have to worry about parents.) Above all, they had that literary desire to participate in extreme experience.

Take, for example, one of the great works of American literature, *The Enormous Room,* by the poet e. e. cummings. When cummings went to Europe as an ambulance driver, he was utterly cynical about the French. He refused to say that the Germans were terrible, which the French authorities wanted him to, and because of a critical letter his friend Slater Brown had been writing they both got arrested. Out of this experience came that marvelous book, one of the first great books about the concentration-camp world. But when you read *The Enormous Room* now, the thing that strikes you is how fresh it is. It's full of energy. I've just reread the whole of Dos Passos' famous trilogy, *U.S.A.* The parts about the war are a constant record of carousal—of drinking, lovemaking, roaring through the streets of Paris and elsewhere. Dos Passos obviously had a great time.

When did disillusionment begin to affect their fiction, and why?

When they began to look at the world after the Versailles Treaty, and especially when they began to look at the leadership we were getting under Harding and Coolidge, they felt, understandably, that an awful lot of people had died for nothing.

I think the greatest thing ever written about the First World War by an American is the prose poem in *U.S.A.* called "The Body of an American," which depicts in a most sardonic and savage way the finding and burial of the Unknown Soldier. It portrays the unctuous hypocrisy of the government in picking out one corpse to honor from among so many. But the point is that it is also an attempt to describe the physical ecstasy of war, both the danger, which is an ecstasy, and the sense of annihilation —triumphing over danger, and then the losing oneself in it. That's why *The Red Badge of Courage* is such a great book; it describes war as if it were a sexual encounter.

Of course Hemingway's *A Farewell to Arms* is very sentimental and romantic about this kind of experience. But then Hemingway always was sentimental, as well as the most self-centered of all American novelists. He was a brilliant lyricist, but he could never write a really fine novel. He captured perfectly one level of the physical experience of war because he was perhaps the most wounded writer of our time. He suffered a whole series of wounds and catastrophes in the war, and he described them with physical immediacy.

You once wrote that Hemingway "brought a major art to a minor vision of life." Would you elaborate on this thought?

Well, I'll take the word "major" away; Hemingway produced an *original* art. He was one of the great painters of prose, a writer of extraordinary freshness. The early stories have a directness and a lyric vibration which is absolutely incomparable. He was the most original stylist of his period. The "minor vision of life," of course, resulted from his self-centeredness. Hemingway's career is depressing because he could only return to early experiences. He was very much preoccupied with his own

wounds, and with an image of himself as a virile male that obviously derived from a very great anxiety. He was an original rather than a great writer.

Disillusionment is clearest in Faulkner's early work. Faulkner had volunteered for the Royal Air Force before America entered the war; he was overeager to get involved, and he had some bad experiences in those rickety, primitive planes of 1916. His early work is not as interesting as Hemingway's or Fitzgerald's, however. Yet he developed in the 1920's a whole series of truly Balzacian novels—perhaps the only Balzacian novels in American fiction—about a whole region, the South. He was able to do this because of his marvelous sense of contrast between the popular image of the South and the reality. Of course, he had, unlike the northern writers, many different groups to write about. No other American novelist had such a range of types and classes to choose from— the aristocracy, the low peasant class, and the Negroes and Indians. This gave his work the human contrast and differentiation that didn't exist in St. Paul, Minnesota, or Oak Park, Illinois.

Certainly any other southern novelist, of whom there were many, would have had the same opportunity?

Mississippi was and is special because it was so poor, because it was so full of illusion. It had been a frontier territory for a long time. In "The Bear," one of the greatest stories ever written, when Faulkner describes the wilderness and the hunting, you realize that a physical frontier still existed, and the effect is fantastic. There was also tremendous provincialism in Mississippi, and of course

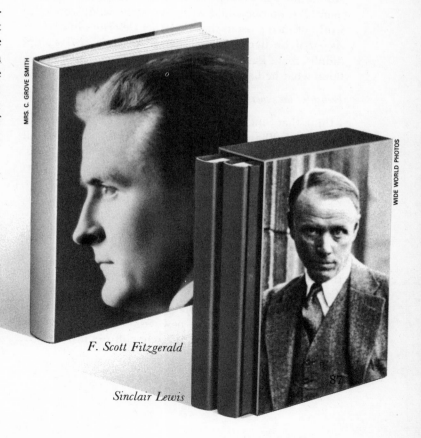

MRS. C. GROVE SMITH

WIDE WORLD PHOTOS

F. Scott Fitzgerald

Sinclair Lewis

87

Ernest Hemingway

John Dos Passos

William Faulkner

the excess of Negroes over whites created for the whites an atmosphere of danger, hostility, and tension. And Faulkner also evokes the feeling, oddly enough, of being close to the Middle West, which in many ways allies Faulkner to Mark Twain and also to contemporaries of his own like Dos Passos and Sinclair Lewis.

It seems to me you're attributing Faulkner's greatness exclusively to the environment he lived in.

Not at all! I'm saying that he seized upon that environment. But no one could write about the wild, wonderful world of race passion that Faulkner describes in *Light in August* if he lived in Richmond, Virginia. Mississippi didn't create Faulkner. Faulkner had the talent to seize upon what he had around him.

Which of the other writers of the 1920's seem to you important?

I think that Sinclair Lewis was a very important writer. He was a brilliant satirist and social critic, but above all he had, like H. L. Mencken, a very strong sense of values, a very solid point of view. In his best books—*Main Street* and *Babbitt*—but even in *Dodsworth*, he presented a dissection of American materialism and cultural sterility. Only after the Depression, when Lewis lost that sharp-edged point of view, did he stop being interesting as a writer. Lewis is easy to underestimate; his achievement is very hard to pin down. He had an enormous influence on the American mind. Indeed, many of these novelists of the 1920's had great impact on their society. Dos Passos, Hemingway, Lewis, and Fitzgerald became creators of a new language, of a whole new vision of society. They made readers aware of two different cultures in America:

the middle-class culture, which was satirized so bitingly by Lewis, and the "ideal" culture of the intelligentsia. And to a degree they changed how readers looked at these cultures and thus the cultures themselves. Henry James was widely read and influential in that sense, but he did not shape the beliefs and attitudes of readers the way Lewis, a lesser writer surely, shaped them.

Why was this so?

Because the characteristic point of view of James, and of Howells, was ethical. James's greatest stories were about individual conscience winning over social institutions. But the characteristic note of Lewis' fiction was his sardonic, subversive feeling about American mores, which was easy for the reader to catch. It requires a very delicate kind of imaginative sympathy to read James's *Portrait of a Lady*, for example, and feel that a basic problem of American society is being described. One must identify completely with Isabel Archer, which takes some doing, to recognize the complex and subtle moral world in which she's involved. But when Lewis describes Babbitt in his office, fumbling over the writing of a letter and having a secretary finally write it herself, when Lewis portrays the American businessman as essentially an inefficient parasite, almost any American can recognize the type. Very simply, Lewis dealt with social patterns, social fables—with *groups*. Even Fitzgerald, who was in many ways the most exquisite American novelist after James, was concerned with group behavior, whereas the only group portrayed by James was the American elect.

Again and again, looking back upon these writers of the twenties, I see that Faulkner, Fitzgerald, Lewis, Dos

Passos, and Hemingway each did something quite remarkable. None of them was like anybody else. There has never been anyone remotely like Sinclair Lewis. That is true also of the romantic Fitzgerald, of the utterly idiosyncratic Faulkner, of Hemingway. Or consider Dos Passos. Today, no critic takes him seriously. But read *U.S.A.* There is nothing remotely resembling Dos Passos' method, his tone, his color, his vocabulary. He is absolutely his own man. And that, of course, is a great thing.

Why did so many of these writers of the 1920's deteriorate in their later careers?

Well, remember Fitzgerald's great remark, that there are no second acts in American life. If anything, deterioration is the rule rather than the exception. American writers are famous for early brilliance, and then for petering out. Ever since Mark Twain, the successful American novelist has also become a celebrity, a prima donna, and in a way an economic royalist. Mark Twain was a rich man; Lewis and Hemingway and others became very rich through their work. Successful American novelists have a peculiar relation with the public, very much like that of a movie star. They tend to become too much concerned with fame. Hemingway became so interested in reaching a big audience that after a while he couldn't write at all.

How about Faulkner?

Faulkner did not wear out, but one reason was that he didn't live in a big city. Remember also that Faulkner did not become successful until relatively late in his career. Unlike Hemingway and Fitzgerald, both of them great best sellers, Faulkner did not catch on with the public. He was able to withstand success because he didn't have any for a long time.

F. Scott Fitzgerald, from the moment he published his first book, *This Side of Paradise*, was a great celebrity. He conducted his love affair with his wife—which is a very tragic story—in public. He felt he had to make a lot of money. When he couldn't make it writing novels, he wrote short stories for the *Saturday Evening Post*, being paid five or six thousand dollars for a story he would turn out in two or three days. But he never had enough money or enough praise. So he began to drink heavily. (Liquor, by the way, was a problem for all these writers.)

How did the Great Depression affect American writers?

The influence of the 1920's lasted pretty much until the middle 1930's, when the experimental, avant-garde side of the twenties petered out. As to the Depression itself, it produced some good novelists, like James T. Farrell, Richard Wright, and Nathanael West, whose *Miss Lonelyhearts* is important. But many writers got caught up in ideological issues, which in general lessened their artistic achievements. Only a very great writer like Faulkner was able to withstand the pressure of constant leftist criticizing. Properly speaking, the American novelist didn't get back to himself, as an independent creator, until after World War II. By and large, the 1930's was a period in which many writers sacrificed their individuality, became more conscious of society than of themselves.

If World War I was the greatest political event of the early twentieth century, wasn't the Great Depression the most important socioeconomic event of the era? Did it not have an impact on literature comparable to that of World War I?

No. The reason why the First World War produced such a brilliant body of American novelists and books was that the writers were all upper-middle-class; the war for them was a great chance of breaking with their backgrounds. What the Depression did for American literature was to awaken literary recognition on the part of people from the immigrant groups in the big cities. The typical writer of the 1920's was someone from a "good family," like cummings, whose father was a minister; Hemingway, whose father was a doctor; Dos Passos, whose father was a lawyer. The typical writer of the 1930's, however, was someone like Richard Wright, whose father was a tenant farmer; Ralph Ellison, whose father was a poor Negro in Oklahoma; John Steinbeck, who worked as a bricklayer.

The Depression era saw a remarkable coming-of-age of Jewish, Negro, and Irish writers. (Dreiser was the first important American writer who was not a Protestant and not, properly speaking, middle-class.) Middle-class attitudes had absolutely dominated American fiction. Suddenly this changed. In literature nothing is more im-

Norman Mailer

Saul Bellow

portant than childhood—that's when the vital social experiences that shape us all occur. With the middle-class writer, life provides a sense of balance and poise and subtlety, but it does not provide the direct assault of harsh experience which is so important. After the Depression and World War II there suddenly burst forth a passionate, brilliant school of writers—Jewish, Negro, Irish—who became perhaps the dominant force in contemporary American literary experience.

The Depression and the Second World War were intimately related; after all, the Depression did not end until war broke out. Yet the Second World War did not produce many great novels, and for very clear reasons. The middle-class writers of the twenties went from protected, sheltered homes—from a world still full of the belief in American destiny—to the shattering experiences of the war. But the people of my generation who went to the war from the Depression had no illusions. The war seemed to us neither just nor unjust, but merely a horrible necessity. It also follows that the people who wrote after the Second World War were not middle-class, not interested in forms the way Hemingway and Dos Passos were, not as sophisticated artistically, and not very often as original. Steinbeck wrote one or two quite good books, but he was not as interesting a writer as Hemingway or Dos Passos. There is nothing in the least original, artistically, in *The Grapes of Wrath;* it is simply a true, forceful book. No new forms were developed. Norman Mailer's first book, *The Naked and the Dead*, was modelled on Dos Passos and Hemingway. It was not in the least original, though it's a good book.

Do you mean that modern conditions do not provide a favorable environment for creative writers?

That is, I suppose, the most important question one can ask about the current literary situation. Novelists, of course, enjoy living well and having money, but they cannot keep from feeling morally and intellectually that things are wrong with our society. There is a contradiction between the enormous wealth and splendor of American life and the sense of anxiety, of something fundamentally immoral going on in our society today. A lot of people are able to delude themselves that they are living in the best of all possible worlds, but the novelist, if he's a real writer, senses that things are not right. A writer like Saul Bellow, for example, whom I think very highly of, is a very successful American. He has a position of great honor, and he certainly enjoys all the fruits of living in our intoxicating century. Yet his work is full of the most terrible sense of grief, of guilt, of foreboding. Why is this? Because in this privileged world human relationships are deteriorating. Bellow is aware, I would assume, that we have a civilization but not a culture, a society without standards. He recognizes that something

about the very nature of modern society makes for great destructiveness. This awareness of man's destructiveness has become more intense as a result of the Second World War. You cannot kill thirty million people and then expect that the world will go back to normal and that sensitive writers will say: "Life is great."

Does Norman Mailer's work reflect something of the same view—that modern society is destructive, that "things are not right"?

Yes. Mailer is an extraordinarily talented man. He has a very muscular, combative kind of talent, and he completely understands and rejoices in the popular side of American life. In what I think is his best book, *The Armies of the Night*, he says that he even felt a sneaking sympathy for the federal marshals in Washington opposing the pickets (of whom he was one), because he recognized in them the same comic, sardonic talent which he had found among the men he had known in the Army. Like Stephen Crane, he has a great passion for what happens in the street, in crowds. At the same time, of course, Mailer is also a very interesting ideologist. More than any other good novelist that I can think of, he openly declared after the war that the next chapter in the American imagination would have to deal with a whole new attitude toward sex. His point was that white middle-class men had deprived themselves of certain fundamental qualities of passion. In a famous essay called "The White Negro" he compared the active, strong, reckless quality of the Negro, who as a kind of outlaw in American society had to gain his way by forceful means, with the timid and obedient white middle-class American.

As a novelist, Mailer has been extremely erratic. He has shown himself to be almost uninterested in finishing books properly. But I think he is an original, in many ways the most original, American novelist since Scott Fitzgerald. He reminds me always of Crane and Fitzgerald. He's very sophisticated, but very passionate, very strong, and he also has an extraordinary sense of mischief. The best thing about Mailer is that he has recognized that in our time a strong talent is literally subversive. He has social intelligence of a very prophetic kind.

Twentieth-century America has produced some of the most extraordinary capacities for unhappiness the world has ever seen. And the best novelists have called the score properly on what is happening. The novel as a literary creation deals with the human soul in active relationships, and these are enough to make one despair sometimes. The easy confidence which Americans were supposed to feel has quite departed. I don't know anyone who doesn't live with a sense of anxiety and foreboding because of the violent animosities of our time. And this is where the modern novel really succeeds—in describing human beings and their capacity for destruction.

At the dedication ceremonies, Wilson
hid his disappointment from Carnegie
behind a mask of academic hospitality.

BROWN BROTHERS

What Princeton Really Needed

By JOSEPH FRAZIER WALL

*When Andrew Carnegie was applying the same vigor to giving
away money as he had devoted to making it, Woodrow Wilson,
the president of Princeton University, invited him to visit the
school. Wilson had grandiose plans for Princeton, and he hoped
that the steel-magnate-turned-philanthropist would co-operate.
But what Carnegie decided to bestow is related in this excerpt
from Joseph Frazier Wall's biography* Andrew Carnegie, *which
will be published this fall by Oxford University Press.*

Elected president of the university in June, 1902, Woodrow Wilson almost at once began a campaign to capture
Andrew Carnegie. It would be a most impressive feat
with which to inaugurate his presidency if he could succeed where such old hands in the presidential game of
fund-raising as Butler, White, Gilman, and Eliot had
failed. Early in the spring of his first year in office he
wrote Carnegie a long letter about Princeton and its
needs. He laid great stress upon Princeton's "Scottish
connections" from President John Witherspoon on, although he was wise enough not to stress Princeton's
Presbyterian heritage. "She has been largely made by
Scotsmen, being myself of pure Scots blood, it heartens
me to emphasize the fact." Having, he hoped, established the right ancestral connections, Wilson outlined

the areas of need for Princeton in which Carnegie's
money could be put to good use. He suggested a grad-
uate-college residence system, a school of science, the
introduction of the tutorial system, and a school of
jurisprudence and government, which he outlined as
follows:

My idea would be to make it a school of law, but not in any
narrow or technical sense: a school, rather, in which law and
institutions would be interpreted as instruments of peace, of
freedom, and of the advancement of civilization: international
law as the means and guarantee of cordial understandings
between the nations of the world, private law as the accommodation of otherwise hostile interests, government as the
means of progress. No doubt it would be wise, too, as immediately collateral matter, to expound the part which commerce
and industry have played and must increasingly play, in making for international as well as national peace and for the pro-
motion of all the common interests of mankind. [Wilson apparently believed that if a salmon was too cautious to catch with a
lure, use a net. Almost every Carnegie cliché of the last twenty
years was woven into that mesh.]

He then urged Carnegie to come down to Princeton,
look the school over, and talk further with him on all
of these points.

After much further cajoling, Wilson finally got Carnegie down to Princeton in 1904. Accompanied by trustee Grover Cleveland, who had on his own been doing a little soliciting of Carnegie in behalf of the Princeton graduate school, Wilson gave Carnegie the grand tour of Old Nassau, pointing out the inadequate library and science facilities, going over plans for new graduate-school facilities, introducing him to deans, professors, and bright young Princeton scholars. Carnegie was most amiable, most interested in everything that was shown him. Wilson should have been forewarned of trouble, however, when Carnegie seemed to give undue attention to the physical-education facilities, particularly those used by the varsity football team. Such questions as How many boys play football, How many casualties do you have in a year, etc., were not, if asked by Carnegie, mere efforts at small talk. They were instead related to Carnegie's latest fancy regarding higher education, a crusade to end the playing of football on college campuses—an idea which most American college alumni would find far more heretical than his earlier attacks upon the classics. One strong bond between Carnegie and President Charles William Eliot of Harvard was their common aversion to football. "I should like very much to have the paragraph in which you sum up the faults of that bloody game," Carnegie had written Eliot. "It begins by stating that the maimed and the killed are not the worst feature, it is the trickery, fraud, etc., the plot to concentrate and disable certain players on the other side, etc., that make the game so objectionable." A favorite poetic line, taking care of both Britain and the United States, which Carnegie delighted in quoting was: "The flanelled fools at the wicket/The muddied Oafs at the goal." Wilson would have been well advised to have steered Carnegie far away from the playing fields of Princeton. At the conclusion of the long day, when Carnegie was at last ready to board that quaint vehicle posing as a train to take Princeton visitors back to the main line to New York and Philadelphia, he turned to Wilson and thanked him for a most instructive day. As the story would later be told by generations of delighted Princeton fans, Carnegie then said, "I know exactly what Princeton needs and I intend to give it to her." His momentarily ecstatic host, who had visions of libraries, laboratories, and law schools

Carnegie, pleased with himself for thinking of the unusual gift to the school, did not seem to notice the apparent pain in Wilson's smile.

dancing in his head, eagerly asked, "What?"

"It's a lake. Princeton should have a rowing crew to compete with Harvard, Yale, and Columbia. That will take young men's minds off football."

Carnegie was as good as his word. Construction was begun that spring by the Hudson Engineering Company to build Lake Carnegie by damming up Stony Brook, east of the campus. Howard Russell Butler, Princeton class of '72 and an avid rowing enthusiast, served as general manager of the project. Two and a half years later, at a cost of $400,000, the lake, three and one half miles long, four hundred to one thousand feet wide, was completed and officially opened at elaborate ceremonies attended by Carnegie on December 5, 1906. President Wilson gave a long speech of welcome to Carnegie, concluding with an account of how Carnegie had visited Princeton and had "seen exactly what Princeton needed—a lake." That Wilson could say this with a perfectly straight face was a tribute to his Calvinist upbringing and an indication of how adept college presidents must become in dealing with the eccentricities of wealthy patrons. Carnegie also gave a speech at this momentous occasion in the history of Princeton. He said he had been happy to give the lake in the hope that it would be used for aquatic sports to the discouragement of football. "I have never seen a football game, but I have glanced at pictures of such games, and to me the spectacle of educated young men rolling over one another in the dirt was —well, not gentlemanly."

According to the newspaper reporters who were present, "Mr. Carnegie's remarks were received with murmurs of dissent from the undergraduates." Carnegie, however, was very much pleased with both his gift and speech. He wrote to Charles Eliot, "I did what I could at Princeton to stand by your side in regard to football, and I am happy to say that everybody, from President Cleveland down, thanked me for speaking the needed word." President Eliot, in a rather neat bit of one-upmanship over his Ivy League competitor, promptly replied, "It is odd that your note of yesterday should reach me the day after Harvard won from Yale in debating. Six years ago when I was in Bermuda you congratulated me in winning in debate when we lost in football. The same thing has been repeated this year. We also won in chess."

"HERE IN NEVADA A TERRIBLE CRIME…"

By ALVIN M. JOSEPHY, JR.

Mud flats along a receding shore line show the tragedy of Pyramid Lake, one of the West's great natural wonders. Owned by Indians, it is going down, robbed of the water it needs by a Bureau of Reclamation irrigation project.

93

On January 10, 1844, Lieutenant John C. Frémont of the Corps of Topographical Engineers, exploring southward from Oregon at the head of a party of twenty-five men, reached the summit of a range of barren hills in present-day northwestern Nevada and sighted a large body of water in the desert, "a sheet of green" breaking "upon our eyes like the ocean." "The waves were curling in the breeze," he reported, "and their dark-green color showed it to be a body of deep water. For a long time we sat enjoying the view. . . . It was set like a gem in the mountains."

Frémont and his men found a well-used Indian trail and, following it south along the eastern shore of the great inland lake, passed herds of mountain sheep, flocks of ducks, and odd tufa formations—calcium carbonate deposits precipitated from the water along the lake edge mostly by the timeless action of algae and waves, and resembling castles, domes, and needles of varicolored stone. One of them particularly, an island rising almost three hundred feet above the surface of the water, caught their fancy. It "presented a pretty exact outline of the great pyramid of Cheops," Frémont said. "This striking feature suggested a name for the lake, and I called it Pyramid Lake."

At the south end of the lake the explorers found a village of Northern Paiute Indians who greeted them in friendship and brought them great quantities of fish—"magnificent salmon trout," said Frémont's cartographer, Charles Preuss, who wrote in his diary, "I gorged myself until I almost choked." The fish were giant Lahontan cutthroat trout, a species found in no other part of the world. "Their flavor was excellent," Frémont reported, "superior, in fact, to that of any fish I have ever known. They were of extraordinary size—about as large as the Columbia River salmon—generally from two to four feet in length." There were ample supplies of them, taken from the lake and a river that flowed into it, and the Indians, whom Frémont noted "appeared to live an easy and happy life," gave the newcomers "a salmon-trout feast as is seldom seen . . . every variety of manner in which fish could be prepared—boiled, fried, and roasted in the ashes—was put into requisition; and every few minutes an Indian would be seen running off to spear a fresh one."

The pyramid rose as an island less than three hundred feet above the water when one of Frémont's men sketched it in 1844 (above left). In 1867 photographer Timothy O'Sullivan showed it unchanged (above right). Now, below, it is attached to the shore and looms 365 feet above visitors' cars.

94

That was a century and a quarter ago. To the modern-day visitor who catches his first sight of the huge body of water in the desert, Pyramid Lake is still as breathtakingly dramatic as it was to Frémont. Shaped like a partly opened fan, a little more than thirty miles long on its north-south axis, some eleven miles wide at its broadest expanse in the north and less than four miles wide in the south, it lies in a long, hidden basin in northwestern Nevada near the California border. Ranges of barren mountains, rising as high as four thousand feet above the water, surround the lake, descending toward it in steep declines and long, sloping benches and flats covered with sagebrush and other desert plants. On the south the mountains conceal the lake from travellers hurrying by on the east-west railroad or Interstate 80, as well as from the growing urban centers of Reno and Sparks, only thirty miles to the southwest.

The color of the lake, deep blue, green, or gray, changes to reflect the hues of the desert sky but depends also on the density and movement of concentrations of plankton in its waters. Along the shore there are still few signs of development or of man's presence, and the great sheet of water and hills around it are overwhelmingly quiet save for the sounds of wildlife. California gulls, Caspian terns, and blue herons flap and soar across the sky. Ducks ride the swells, and approximately 7,500 white pelicans, probably the largest colony of that species in North America, nest on Anaho Island, a 750-acre National Wildlife Refuge three hundred yards off the eastern shore. The curled-horned mountain sheep that Frémont saw are gone, but coyotes, mule deer, jack rabbits, and bobcats are abundant, as are armies of ground squirrels, lizards, and other rodents and reptiles that make their home in the desert cover.

The National Park Service has called Pyramid Lake "the most beautiful desert lake in the United States. . . . perhaps the most beautiful of its kind in North America"; conservationists and lovers of outdoor beauty regard its wild solitudes as one of the few remaining unspoiled natural wonders in the American West; and the state of Nevada touts the lake as among its prized attractions for tourists and sportsmen. Yet today the lake is threatened with wanton destruction, the

victim of a uniquely unsavory case of the plundering of natural resources.

A remnant of a larger prehistoric body of water known as Lake Lahontan that filled much of the western Great Basin during the Ice Age, Pyramid Lake has only one principal source of water, the Truckee River, which starts at Lake Tahoe in the High Sierras on the Nevada-California border, almost one hundred miles to the southwest. Pyramid has a maximum depth of about 335 feet, and no outlet, but it loses approximately 147 billion gallons, or about four and a half feet, of water a year by evaporation. It receives a small amount of water from underground sources, from surface run-off, and from occasional desert rains; but in the main it has depended on the Truckee River, which historically kept it at a somewhat fixed level.

In 1905, however, the Reclamation Service of the Department of the Interior built Derby Dam across the Truckee twenty miles east of Reno, diverting part of the river away from Pyramid Lake and into a government irrigation project in the Nevada desert around present-day Fallon (see map, page 96). Since then, for sixty-five years, Pyramid Lake has received only that water which Derby Dam did not divert for the irrigation project (known now as the Newlands Project, for Nevada's reclamation-minded Senator Francis G. Newlands).

The results at the lake have been as dramatic as they were predictable. The great sheet of water has dropped an average of one and a fourth feet a year for a total so far of more than eighty feet. Its shoreline recedes an average of ten feet a year; a sister body of water, Lake Winnemucca, once also about thirty miles long and fed by overflow water from Pyramid Lake, has entirely dried up and disappeared. Pyramid Lake's length has shrunk by several miles, and its surface area has contracted by more than fifty square miles. Frémont's pyramid, now rising 365 feet above the lake, is no longer an island but is connected to the shore; and Anaho Island, facing the same prospect, will surely lose its famed pelicans, once coyotes and other predators can cross on dry land to the rookeries.

At the south end of the lake sandbars almost clog the mouth of the Truckee, so that fish can no longer get up the river

to spawn. As a result, the unique giant Lahontan cutthroats described by Frémont—once so numerous that Pyramid was world-famous as a fishery, containing probably the biggest concentration of large fish of any body of water on the continent—disappeared from the lake about 1938. Another fish, known as the cui-ui (pronounced *kwee-wee*) and also found nowhere else on earth, is still abundant in the lake. A valuable food fish, growing up to nine pounds, it too now faces extinction.

The lake may never vanish altogether; someday it will have shrunk small enough, probably to about 70 per cent of its present size, that the inflow can equal the decreased evaporation and stabilize the lake's level. But by then, some hydrologists maintain, the water will be too saline for fish, and Pyramid will be a dead salt lake, or so close to it that its preservation, even at that level, will no longer be worthwhile. The Bureau of Reclamation, which still must see that Truckee River water is diverted to the irrigation project that it built, does not admit to this ultimate prospect but suggests only that as Pyramid Lake's level declines and its salinity increases, "there will be some change in the fishery."

All those facts, however, dismal as they may be to those who would save a great natural wonder from destruction, do not, unfortunately, give an inkling of the full—and truly searing—dimensions of what is involved.

"This is one of the blackest pages in the history of American fisheries and represents what must be close to the ultimate in greed and lack of foresight," said Thomas J. Trelease, an official of the Nevada Fish and Game Commission, in 1967. It is "a grim, humiliating sermon in selfishness on one hand and public apathy on the other."

What he was underscoring was the fact that the lake just happens to belong to a small and impoverished tribe of American Indians—some nine hundred members of the Pyramid Lake tribe of Northern Paiutes, descendants of the people who welcomed Frémont in 1844. As Frémont noted, they were people who lived principally on fish, and in 1859 the federal government set aside the lake for them as the main part of an otherwise barren reservation, with the intent that it serve as their major means of existence.

Through the years federal courts confirmed the lake as the Indians' property, and the tribe kept it unspoiled. When the government in 1905 began to divert water from the lake, therefore, it not only took from the Indians something that was legally theirs, but threw into jeopardy the Paiutes' very livelihood.

No one in 1905 appears to have considered what would happen to the reservation or to the people who lived on it, once their water was taken from them. No one consulted the Indians or asked them for the water—despite the fact that with first-priority water rights, going back to 1859, they could have claimed adequate water for the lake. No one even told them that the water was going to be taken. In plain words, the water was stolen from them in an all-too-common repetition of a fate suffered by other tribes in the arid West.

Ironically, moreover, the action on the Truckee River in 1905 was carried out by the same agency of the federal government charged by law to *protect* the Indians' rights and property, the Department of the Interior. Voiceless and powerless in a white man's world, the Paiutes were in every sense of the word wards of the government. But when Nevada's political leaders asked Congress to authorize the irrigation project, the Department of the Interior raised not a murmur in defense of the Indians' water. In a conflict between the interests of the Indians and those of the white farmers who were "opening up" the West, the department's solicitors turned their backs on the "vanishing race."

That might have been the end of the story, except that the Pyramid Lake Paiutes did not vanish. In the 1960's the Indians, gaining new voice, unity, and self-assertiveness, began an eleventh-hour fight to save their lake. That struggle, still being waged, is based essentially on a Supreme Court ruling made for other tribes. In 1908 and again in 1963 the Court decided that when the United States government established Indian reservations, it also reserved, by implication, sufficient water in any streams running through a reservation to carry out the purposes of that reservation. Under this so-called Winters' Doctrine (after the name of the 1908 case), the Pyramid Lake Reservation had a first-priority right to all the water necessary for its purposes.

But to date the Department of the Interior, still responding to the Bureau of Reclamation and Nevada's non-Indian pressures rather than to the Paiutes' rights, has compounded its original dereliction of responsibility by refusing to undertake court action for the Indians, and the latter have neither the financial means nor the hydrological and other technical expertise necessary to go to court on their own. Moreover, they have

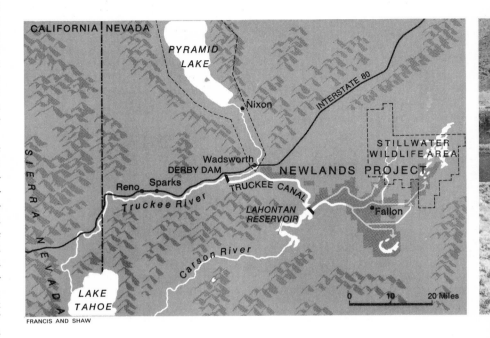

FRANCIS AND SHAW

been kept on the defensive by an unending series of maneuvers on the part of white water users designed to prevent them, or the federal government as their trustee, from *ever* going to court for more water for Pyramid Lake. A tangle of decrees, statutes, regulations, and water rights and laws have been used to deceive and thwart them, while the Department of the Interior claims that its hands are tied and does nothing.

The Indians view the tortuous fight for their lake not just as a struggle for what rightfully belongs to them but as a matter of life and death. "Land without water is like a body without blood," says their tribal leader, thirty-two-year-old James Vidovich, an electrical worker and descendant of a Paiute who received the family's surname from a Yugoslav employer. Vidovich lives with some five hundred members of his tribe just south

of where the Truckee flows into Pyramid Lake. His people, energetic and self-reliant, have had long association with the whites; save when a trip to town or other occasion calls for a suit, the Indians dress in jeans, boots, and wide-brimmed hats like most other persons in the outdoor areas of Nevada. Their reservation today comprises a total of 475,-086 acres and includes the lake itself (which presently covers 107,900 acres), a

band of barren and mountainous country entirely surrounding it, and a panhandle of land extending about seventeen miles along the lower Truckee. Two small towns, Nixon, where the tribal headquarters are located, and Wadsworth, lie in the panhandle.

Although most of the Indians' land is arid, with irrigation some of the strip south of the lake can be farmed and grazed. So far the Indians have opened somewhat fewer than eight hundred acres of bottomland to irrigation, principally for raising hay for cattle and horses; but the tribe has been unable to afford to irrigate the higher land, and the federal government has yet to grant financial assistance, despite its promise to do so. Moreover, the Paiutes at heart are not farmers or stockmen.

Thus the lake, with its cui-ui and artificially planted fish which must be periodically restocked, is still their major resource, and along with the fish for food, it now provides 75 per cent of their tribal income through the sale of fishing and boating permits to whites. (Other income is derived from cattle and from part-time jobs on ranches or in the cities. Still, in 1967 almost 70 per cent of the Pyramid Lake Paiutes were unemployed, and 52 per cent of their families had incomes under $2,000 a year.) And should

was grossly overestimated, and since its inception, the project has never had more than 50,000–60,000 acres under irrigation with water from both rivers. Sixty-five years after its beginning, the project today looks like an old, settled farm area, with many grassy pastures, fields, gardens, and stands of trees, all watered by canals, and new and old barns and farm and ranch houses shaded by trees and fronting on the highways

and sheep are brought in from the ranges to be fattened for market. In addition, some farmers maintain dairy herds, raise turkeys and other poultry, and keep bees. Most of the people, typically industrious, middle-income farm families, live on the lands of the project, but many who own uneconomic one- and two-acre lots with water rights lease their land to bigger operators and live in Fallon. The latter, with a population close to three thou-

BUREAU OF RECLAMATION, DEPARTMENT OF THE INTERIOR

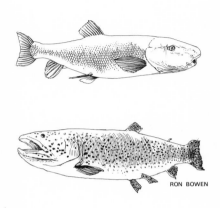

RON BOWEN

At left is the culprit, Derby Dam, seen diverting waters of the Truckee River into a canal (at the bottom of the picture) that runs to the Newlands irrigation project. Water unneeded by the project flows in a diminished stream toward Pyramid Lake. The map shows the course of the Truckee from its Lake Tahoe source. The giant cutthroat trout (top, above) once made Pyramid Lake world-famous but has now vanished from it. The unique cui-ui below it is threatened, as are the white pelicans (right) on Anaho Island in the lake.

U.S. FISH AND WILDLIFE SERVICE

the lake be preserved, there is a new promise for the future: the orderly development of shorefront recreation facilities, strictly controlled by the tribe in limited areas on the lake, can, according to a recent survey, provide steady jobs for the unemployed and make the reservation economically self-sustaining. Outside capital is available for such development, but not for a lake whose shoreline is gradually declining. And so, as the money waits for the lake's decline to be halted, the Paiutes have been pressing their case.

Their principal rival for the Truckee's water, the Newlands Project, was originally planned to irrigate 232,800 acres of desert with water from the Truckee, and another 137,000 acres with water from the Carson River, which runs somewhat parallel to, and south of, the Truckee. The available supply of water, however,

and secondary roads that lace the district. Except at its edges, where the project borders on sagebrush desert and muddy flats where temporary flooding occurs, a visitor might imagine he was almost anywhere in the rural Midwest.

Altogether, the water diverted from the Truckee to the project serves about 1,025 farms on which dwell approximately 5,800 people. The farmers produce mainly alfalfa and hay for cattle; some barley, wheat, and other grains; corn silage; and a small amount of vegetables and fruits, including potatoes and melons. In the winter thousands of cattle

sand, is the principal shopping and marketing town on the project and, except for a garish gambling casino, might, with its wide streets and easy, friendly pace, pass for any county seat in the agricultural West.

The average gross crop value of the Newlands Project amounts to no more than $4,500,000 per year, and from 1909 until 1965 the value of all crops produced during those fifty-six years totalled only $104,500,000. These figures assume significance when matched as achievements of "progress" against what is being denied to the Indians. If the decline of the lake were halted and recreational facilities built on its shores, for instance, it is estimated that recreational income at the lake would soon exceed the annual crop value of the irrigation project and that within fifteen years this income would increase to more than three times

97

the annual value of the project.

Most people on the project are not unsympathetic to the plight of Pyramid Lake, but they argue bitterly that they and their families have long since acquired legal rights to the water, and it is just too bad if there is not enough in the Truckee for the lake as well. One of the largest landowners on the project, Carl F. Dodge, a Nevada state senator whose 1,400 acres have been owned by his family for fifty years, reflects the attitude of many. If the water is more valuable for the purpose of keeping Pyramid Lake alive than for keeping the project's farms fertile, Dodge said, "then let them buy the water rights and take them over. All I can say about it is if they feel that way, money talks."

No one, as yet anyhow, believes that such a course is economically or, in Nevada, politically practicable. Ranchers and farmers form a powerful element in the state's political life, and with few areas in Nevada able to support agriculture, it is a safe bet that the state would vigorously resist permitting one of its biggest and richest agricultural districts to return to desert. Moreover, the farms are no longer the only users of the project's water. Through the years, "tailwater" draining off the farms built up previously existing marshes in the adjoining desert. Like Pyramid Lake, these became the habitat of large flocks of ducks and other waterfowl and attracted gun clubs. At the same time, other waste water created a partly irrigated pasture, which farmers of the project put to use as a common grazing ground. In 1948 the Department of the Interior's Fish and Wildlife Service made a pact with the irrigators on the Newlands Project and Nevada's Fish and Game Commission. Out of the waterfowl marshlands were created the Stillwater Wildlife Management area (a public shooting ground) and the Stillwater National Wildlife Refuge (a protected area), and the Interior Department also agreed to develop and improve the pasture. Once established, both the wildlife area and the pasture became recognized "users" of Truckee water. The effect up to now, therefore, has been to provide water for Stillwater ducks and project cows, while continuing to deny it to the Indians and Pyramid Lake. And in still another development a large storage reservoir built

on the project has begun to thrive as a recreational center. The very water diverted away from the Indians' lake is now being used by whites for recreation on an artificial lake less than thirty-five miles away.

All of this must be reckoned with by the Indians in their late-hour attempt to save Pyramid Lake, and it is further complicated by non-Indian users of water upstream from the lake on both the Truckee and the Carson. The number of these users, including other farmers as

In 1925 a world record forty-one-pound native cutthroat was taken from Pyramid Lake. Since their disappearance, anglers like this Indian father and son try for artificially stocked species.

well as domestic and industrial interests around Reno, has increased greatly since 1905, and not surprisingly their competitive claims to the limited supply of water have grown more complex. But the Paiutes' determined fight is beginning to loom as an ominous threat to all non-Indian users—capable, perhaps, of unsettling many, if not all, of the established water rights on the two rivers. The result has been to increase white irritation with the Paiutes. Battle lines have been sharply defined, and added pressure has been brought on both the state government and the Bureau of Reclama-

tion by the white farmers and ranchers to see to it that their water rights are safeguarded.

On the Truckee those rights were firmly established in 1944 by a federal district court decision known as the Orr Water Ditch Company decree. The Department of the Interior did represent the Paiutes at that time but actually worsened the Indians' position by permitting what amounted to the legalization of Pyramid Lake's destruction. The Winters' Doctrine (the 1908 Supreme Court decision) had been in existence for nearly forty years; the department clearly had the opportunity to right an old wrong by insisting on a court grant of adequate water for the lake. But the department asked for no water right at all for the lake, and it got none. The decree gave the Indians a right to only a meager amount of water, but with the provision that it could be used only for irrigation or stock and domestic purposes. (The department's Bureau of Indian Affairs wanted to turn the Paiutes into farmers.) Moreover, the amount of water which they could draw was based on how much land they had under irrigation, and since to this day they have been able to irrigate only a strip along the bottomlands, they have never had the legal right to draw more than a fifth of the water granted to them—and none of it, legally, could be used for Pyramid Lake!

In actuality, Pyramid Lake continued to receive water from springs and underground sources below Derby Dam, from leaks in the dam and the first section of the project's canal, and particularly

The Northern Paiute owners of Pyramid Lake, photographed above about 1867, greeted John Frémont in friendship, but they later fought hard and beat the militia when miners overran their land.

from floodwater which the Newlands Project could not use and which was released from the dam to the lower Truckee. Under the Orr Ditch decree, however, the Indians had no right even to the floodwater, and so in 1955, when the Bureau of Reclamation announced plans to build flood-control dams on the headwaters of the Truckee and Carson rivers, it stated specifically that none of the project's water would be made available to the Indians. This was too much for the Paiutes. On their own, they took their case to the Interior and Insular Affairs committees of both the House and Senate, which were then considering the Washoe Project, of which the new flood-control dams were a part. Both committees responded with reports that noted officially for the first time that Pyramid Lake's crisis was due largely to acts of the federal government, and that the government had never undertaken compensatory measures to maintain the fishery of the lake and now ought to do so. When the bill authorizing the project passed Congress on August 1, 1956, it directed that facilities be provided to increase water releases to Pyramid Lake to restore its fishery.

By 1963, however, when the Bureau of Reclamation finally firmed up its plans for the project, it revealed, on the contrary, that the new dams would cause the lake to go down even faster. In April, 1964, responding to protests by the Paiutes, then Secretary of the Interior Stewart Udall appointed a task force to examine the claims of everyone, including the Indians. A preliminary report, completed in September, indicated concern over how to increase, rather than decrease, the water going to Pyramid Lake. It proposed certain modifications in the Washoe plan and economies by the Newlands Project. But it recommended no specified grant of water to the lake, nor did it guarantee that the lake would not suffer from the Washoe Project. It said only that the government should exercise "every effort to maintain the greatest practicable flow of water into Pyramid Lake."

When public hearings on the report were held in Reno, the Paiutes and various Indian and white supporters argued angrily against the omission of a guaranteed grant of water for the lake.

"Why tell us you will give us as much water as possible?" demanded Avery Winnemucca, a spokesman for the Paiutes. "Why don't you be specific? At least you did that with others. You've got figures to prove that there is so much allocation for this and so much for that, all in figures. But Pyramid Lake, no. You give us as much as possible."

Other pro-lake, pro-Indian speakers went further, claiming that any discussion of the Washoe Project was premature until the government, under the Winters' Doctrine, took steps to guarantee the lake's preservation. "Here in Nevada a terrible crime has been committed against Nevada's first citizens," charged the Reverend H. Clyde Mathews, chairman of the Nevada Advisory Committee to the United States Commission on Civil Rights. Then he added what few others in Nevada had previously admitted openly:

If this property had been owned by six hundred white stockholders in an irrigation company, would this property have been taken without compensation, *or at all?* . . . The United States government itself has been discriminatory on the basis of race, creed, and national origin in the manner in which the Nevada Indians' water and fishery rights have been allowed to be denied, ignored, manipulated, and in effect destroyed.

Despite such pleas, the task force's final report refused to recommend that the government go to court to seek a water grant for the lake. There was no time for a long, complex water-rights case. A water-users' vote on the Washoe Project was waiting. Moreover, this was a classic illustration of how American Indians have suffered from having their affairs handled by the Department of the Interior. The department chose the course of action that avoided an internal conflict of mammoth proportions: the successful prosecution of the Indians' case would have endangered not only the Newlands Project but other reclamation projects that Indian tribes elsewhere might claim had overridden their rights.

All the Department of the Interior could do for Pyramid Lake, the task force noted, was to undertake certain measures—including the salvaging of excess water, the elimination of waste, and the imposition of regulations and controls at the Newlands Project—that would increase the amount of water available to the lake. The carrying-out of the recommendations would guarantee a considerable increase of water to the lake, Udall told the Indians, and with that promise they withdrew their opposition to the Washoe Project. On November 3, 1964, the voters in the affected Nevada river basins approved it.

The government did make efforts to conserve Truckee River water by setting up certain controls on the Newlands Project, but it soon became questionable whether the Indians would benefit. Despite the Paiutes' appeals for a statement of a legal basis for the water Udall had promised them, the Department of the Interior refused to assert that the United States owned, controlled, and had the right to deliver to Pyramid Lake the water it was going to save on the Newlands Project, thus leaving that water open to appropriation by non-Indian users.

In 1968 the threat surfaced with a vengeance. Since 1955 California and Nevada had been working on a settlement that would divide between the two states the waters flowing from Lake Tahoe. All the water in question (including the Truckee and Carson) passed through California before entering Nevada, so California, too, had a claim to it. After thirteen years of work, a document was drafted that not only limited the Indians' water to what the Orr Ditch decree gave them in 1944, but *went beyond that by expressly preventing the federal government and the Indians from ever going to court to seek more water for Pyramid Lake.* Henceforth, the Indians would have to apply to Nevada for any water saved by the Newlands Project, and the threat of the Winters' Doctrine would disappear.

The compact was too raw even for the Department of the Interior, which did not care to turn over the fate of federal water rights in Nevada to the state. The department registered its objections, with the implied threat that Congress would not ratify the agreement. But the Nevada legislature took up the document all the same, and after brief hearings approved the compact. In California it was a different story. Unwilling to risk rejection by Congress, and appealed to by the Northern Paiute Indians, the National Congress of American Indians, and many Indian and white friends, the California Assembly Committee on Natural Resources and Conservation refused to approve the compact unless it was rewritten to preserve Pyramid Lake and eliminate objections of the Department of the Interior.

The state of Nevada refused to change its mind, and on July 6, last summer, the new Secretary of the Interior, Walter J. Hickel, met at Lake Tahoe with governors Ronald Reagan of California and Paul Laxalt of Nevada to try to break the deadlock. Their solution, announced to the press after a ninety-minute meeting on the lake in the cabin of a cruiser owned by Reno gambler William Harrah, made matters worse. Without consulting the Indians, they had agreed that engineers should hasten Pyramid Lake's gradual decline by draining it down to the level at which it would stabilize.

As Vine Deloria, Jr., Indian author of *Custer Died for Your Sins* and a former executive director of the National Congress of American Indians, put it: "It was the same logic used by the Army to destroy a Vietnamese village—'We had to destroy the village to save it.' It naturally followed that the only way to save Pyramid Lake was to drain it."

The weird proposal, which would have dropped the lake abruptly by 152 feet and left it a salt lake in a huge basin of mudflats, outraged not only the Paiutes, who could not believe that the three governments would commit such a flagrant robbery of their property, but large numbers of non-Indians in Nevada, who suddenly saw Pyramid Lake as a priceless gem of the desert and an important recreation asset for the whole state. The public outcry forced the three officials to drop the plan hurriedly and set up, instead, another task force of federal and state appointees who would try to satisfy the Indians so a new version of the compact could be written. Even that task force got off to a controversial start, however, when Governor Laxalt claimed the right to name the Paiute representative to the body, which the Indians asserted was dominated, anyhow, by the Bureau of Reclamation.

Since that time the Indians' position has worsened. The Paiutes have continued to ask the federal government to live up to its responsibility and go to court in their behalf, but the Department of the Interior has ignored their pleas. Instead, it has indicated a determination to complete its Washoe Project dams on the upper Truckee and Carson rivers *before* an Indian suit, based on the Winters' Doctrine, can halt them. With the project's completion, Pyramid Lake's doom will be sealed, since most of the impounded water—including floodwater that the lake has been receiving up to now—will go to the Newlands irrigators and other non-Indian users. A government-initiated suit for the Indians would be even more unlikely at that time than now, and the lake's future would be decided by the task force. The shape of that decision is already clear: "Obviously," said a Bureau of Reclamation official about the Indians' rights, "there must be some compromises." The lake will still go down.

Facing continued betrayal by the government, the Indians have decided recently to try to go to court for themselves. They lack resources and, perhaps, adequate legal and technical support. But they have shown a determination to seek the means to press the issue.

It is more than a case of asserting their rights, undoing a theft, or saving a lake. "Everywhere you turn there is a reminder of the injustice that was done to [Indians in the past], an injustice of a remote, irreparable, and therefore comfortable, variety," wrote A. J. Liebling in 1955. In Nevada in 1970, to another Indian people, in an injustice neither remote, irreparable, nor comfortable, there is the large matter of survival.

Alvin M. Josephy, Jr., General Editor of the American Heritage Book Division, is author of The Indian Heritage of America (*Knopf, 1968*) *and a frequent writer on current Indian affairs. Last year he wrote a special report on federal-Indian relations for President Nixon.*

A Haunting New Vision of the Little Big Horn

On the high, treeless plains of central Montana this summer the Department of the Interior, the nation's principal conservation agency and custodian (through the National Park Service) of all national historic monuments, will play host to an estimated 275,000 visitors. They will come, as have millions before them, to see and walk "the very ground" upon which occurred what must be the most memorialized single event in American history: the battle fought on Sunday, June 25, 1876, between some four thousand Indians and five companies of U. S. Cavalry—215 men in all—under the command of George Armstrong Custer. But this year's visitors to the Custer Battlefield, unlike their predecessors, will have the chance to take home, for the price of $1.25, a remarkable new souvenir—a ninety-three page, paperbound handbook, prepared by the Park Service and printed by the U. S. Government Printing Office. It is one of the most striking examples of illustrated history to be published by anyone in some time.

The book includes a concise, lucid account of the celebrated Custer "last stand" written by Robert M. Utley, a number of interesting old photographs, and good maps. But what sets it off from the general run of historic handbooks and from all the innumerable paintings, sculptures, beer ads, bottle caps, and cigarette cards that the Custer fight has inspired over the years, are the fifteen pages of powerful and decidedly original illustrations by artist Leonard Baskin, some of which are reproduced here.

The extra money needed to produce such a book was gotten up by a group of private citizens from Billings called the Custer Battlefield Historical and Museum Association. They told the Park Service only that they wanted "a distinguished piece of publishing." The decision to pick Baskin was made by Vincent Gleason, publications director for the Park Service, who with gentle understatement calls the drawings "very non-G.I." In an afterword for the book, Mitchell A. Wilder, head of the Amon Carter Museum in Fort Worth, writes that Baskin "cuts through a century of mediocre, apocryphal pictures to reveal the actors of this tragic drama as they were, not in the event, but in life and death."

Baskin, who teaches art at Smith College and who also designed the handbook, began work on the drawings two years ago. The Indians were what interested him most, he says. ("It was really *their* 'last stand,' if you stop to think about it.") But his extraordinary seated Custer (right), which is also being used as a huge poster by the Park Service, will doubtless stir up more controversy than anything else in the book. ("I was fascinated by his sense of posturing, his sense of dressing up [see cover] and by his incredible mania about himself.") And while historians continue to debate what Custer did or did not do at the Battle of the Little Big Horn, Baskin says simply: "The Indians took him—that's all. And somehow one is glad. He would have made a terrible President."

Two of Baskin's strongest drawings are of General George Crook (above) and of the dead Custer (below). The Indians did in fact strip Custer's corpse, but the Montana sponsors of the book at the last moment considered this drawing unsuitable. As a result it was dropped, and the book has the added curiosity of one entirely blank page.

Had it been specifically designed for the purpose,
says the author, the motorcar could not be doing a better
job of destroying our cities and countryside

THE MOTORCAR
VS. AMERICA

Yesterday's "dreamboats" piling up everywhere are but part of the price we are paying for a national love affair with the motorcar that began about the time th

For the ordinary citizen who can afford one, as most Americans can, the motorcar probably means more than any other single gift of the machine age. It is the magic carpet that makes us master of the world's domains: it is wings; it is speed, it is drama, it is adventure. It is also nirvana in a capsule. Enclosed in its luxurious appointments, in a body-contoured seat, air-conditioned, removed from reality by power brakes and power steering, lulled by the blandishments of various worlds of make-believe piped in by the dashboard radio, we know ourselves cherished and safeguarded as we could hardly expect to be elsewhere this side of the womb.

The motorcar is the fulfillment of pride, an embodiment of rakish elegance specially designed by platoons of experts to put its possessor ahead of the Joneses. It is self-assertion. It is an arrogant

chromed and lacquered torpedo with the throbbing power of three hundred champing horses, the apotheosis of humdrum man, the transformation of the put-upon adolescent into a figure to be reckoned with. Svelte and racy for the female of the species, it is sexual drive incarnate for the male. It is symbolism, and it is sin itself—an ever-available mobile bedroom in which more chastity goes by the board every week than has been undermined by all the erotic books in history.

But the price: that messy business of a price . . .

Perhaps too much should not be made of those fifty-odd thousand lives destroyed and the hundreds of thousands of injured the dreamboat leaves in its wake every year. The subject has become banal. We have lived so long with the slaughter that the victims have become

mere statistics, mere repeated statistics.

Well, not entirely. There is that scene none of us is spared for long: the red light flashing atop the police cruiser, the crumpled cars askew, the splintered glass, the dark stains on the concrete you pray are only gasoline or oil, and—oh no!—the two figures prone on the grass. It is a vivid scene, and no less so in retrospect when your wife is late in getting home or your daughter is out in a motorized missile (the term is an insurance-company president's) with a youth charged by an adolescent's flood of hormones and an impulsive and reckless exhibitionism. (On the test track, says a writer who tried one, the new Ford Torino "loafed around the banked turns at over 115 m.p.h.") Try not to think of it. Just hope that the wives and children slaughtered will once again be someone else's. The mathematical chances are

By CHARLTON OGBURN, JR.

that they will be, and that probability satisfies the public.

But if the public can go along with highway deaths the equal of seven Gettysburgs a year—and I have little doubt that it can and will in time take those of ten or a dozen in its stride—so can civilization. Whether civilization can survive the other costs of the motorcar is the real question.

It is not by mere chance that "civilization" and "city" are inseparably linked etymologically. From the beginning the city has *been* civilization, and the history of civilization is the history of great

AUTOMOBILE MANUFACTURERS ASSOCIATION

oung Quaker tried his hand at the wheel back in 1904.

cities. And what stirring and exalting things great cities are!—Periclean Athens and Renaissance Florence with a few tens of thousands, as well as, I am certain, London, Paris, and Rome with millions. Surely the great city is the outstanding work of man, synthesizing all his other works in an organic whole with a life, vitality, and personality of its own. Historically, human achievements in the arts and in the arts of civilization are clustered in cities; it is in the interaction of those to whom perceptions, ideas, and cultivation of the mind are important that civilization flourishes.

But we need cities for humbler purposes, too. We need frequent and intimate encounters with others to bring out what is latent in us and to draw us out of ourselves. "All the evidence of psychiatry," says sociologist George C. Homans, "shows that membership in a group sus-

tains a man, enables him to bring up children who will in turn be happy and resilient." We are both comforted and kindled by the throng and variety of human beings bent upon their pursuits in the living city. We need that, at least much of the time, as we need the human sounds of the city, the laughter and shouts, the scents of bakeries—all that goes with human lives being lived together, interwoven and juxtaposed.

But the city, as we all know, is now faced with bankruptcy and is hard pressed to provide even the essential services. Life has been withdrawing from its streets, which are increasingly unsafe. Increasingly, we discuss as a real question whether the city can be saved. But what we resist acknowledging is that in the demise of the city the automobile is playing a key role. Indeed the automobile could hardly do a better job of wrecking the city if it had been designed for that specific purpose.

Last summer I returned to my alma mater for the first time in thirty-seven years. The girls with skirts up to their bottoms and the young men made up for an opera with a cast of Balkan banditti or for the Last Supper were novel, decidedly. But what stunned me was the revolution the motorcar had wrought. Gone was the repose, gone the quiet in which reflection takes place, gone any feeling in the air that thought might be important, gone the sense of human community. The Harvard of old was now a collection of diminished and somehow shabby fragments separated by rivers of vehicular traffic. Bumper to bumper, flank to flank, the cars filled the streets, exhausts panting, motors roaring on the change of lights, horns blaring. Trucks and buses yowled and rumbled. Everything seemed incidental to the motorcar, to its racket and din, to its acrid stench, to the tempo of its acceleration, to the tension it engendered, to its power to crush flesh and bone. Which were the drivers and which the driven? If the students, obscurely but profoundly aware of the denigration of human values in the society they saw around them, were difficult to keep in order, we had no right to be surprised.

But of course Cambridge, Massachusetts, was no different from any other segment of urban America. It was simply that on returning I had been transported

in minutes from 1932 to 1969. And the juxtaposition was too much. "Let me out of here," I said to myself, "and don't let me ever come back!"

But I have not been alone in this urge, which is the real point. By the millions the city dwellers *have* been getting out—to the suburbs. The congested streets on which traffic is slower than half a century ago; the danger to life in crossing them, especially to the lives of children; the pall of hydrocarbons; the torrent of noise (the truck routes through Manhattan at three A.M. sound like Panzer divisions on the move); the lack of a sense of space; the loss of peace of mind; the sheer oppression of the spirit under the weight of the endless spectacle of cars—all that and more have been behind the exodus. And the emigrants have been the people of substance who pay taxes and who, having a stake in the proprietorship of the city, could have been expected to fight to preserve it, had they stayed.

The damage the emigrants do by their departure they compound by the manner of their return. For as most of them are wage earners, return they must, every morning. And as far as feasible, or in the absence of choice, they come by the means that offers door-to-door convenience—the motorcar. Because they pour back into the city by the hundreds of thousands, giant freeways are called for. Picture a bulldozer a hundred feet wide levelling everything in its path through the city's outskirts and the city itself and you have the coming of an autobahn— Herr Hitler's one durable legacy. The city suffers a further shrinkage of its tax base as residences and businesses are shovelled out of the way. (In Washington, D.C., for example, where streets and highways already pre-empt 30 per cent of the land, it was estimated a few years ago that additional freeway projects on the drawing boards would cost the city six million dollars a year in lost revenues.)

For an urban freeway the toll of those displaced from their homes can run into the thousands, and since these are generally the poorer inhabitants, who have difficulty relocating, the result can be mass tragedy. (A stretch of freeway but little over a mile long proposed for lower Manhattan would destroy two thousand homes and ten thousand jobs, Jane Jacobs has charged.) The fabric of neighborhoods is torn, the city dismembered by raceways on which the roar of traffic is never stilled; four million cars a day race along the freeways of Los Angeles County, pouring enough fumes into the atmosphere to kill more than a million trees in San Bernardino National Forest sixty miles away. Parks that help make a city livable offer the highway engineer tempting rights of way: Juneau Park in Milwaukee, Overton Park in Memphis, Fairmount Park in Philadelphia, a park along Brandywine Creek in Wilmington, a whole system of green areas in San Antonio, including Brackenridge and Olmos Basin parks, have been or are evidently going to be gutted by freeways, while many others are under threat, including Washington's Glover-Archbold Park and Minneapolis' Minnehaha Park.

To accommodate the commuters' cars, the city's less profitable structures, and especially those centrally located, are turned over to the wrecker, and these are likely to include buildings that have been around longest and speak of the city's continuity and give it personality. (See, for example, the story on the destruction of the historic Amoskeag mills in Manchester, New Hampshire, in AMERICAN HERITAGE, April, 1970.) Where they stood, the light glints on acres of enamelled car tops; Los Angeles, where an estimated two thirds of the downtown area is already devoted to the transit and parking of automobiles, gives a taste of what is in store for all cities. More than ever it is clear who is boss.

By the time it is completed the National System of Interstate and Defense Highways, as it is called, will comprise 42,500 miles of high-speed freeways connecting the nation's principal cities. It will have taken 1.5 million acres in new rights of way and 750,000 pieces of property. The cost will probably be half again as much as the forty billion dollars originally estimated.

For freeways built under the Interstate System, the federal government pays 90 per cent, the state 10. (This contrasts with the fifty-fifty split by which ordinary national highways have been built.) Funds for these come from revenues on the sale of gasoline (four cents a gallon), new trucks, buses and trailers, tires, lubricating oil, truck and bus parts and accessories, and a tax on heavy vehicles. The revenues go into a Highway Trust Fund administered by the Bureau of Public Roads, from which four to five billion dollars a year are paid out for new highways. The process is automatic; the funds flow without stop, year in, year out. Freeways lead to more use of cars, which lead to more freeways. The Asphalt Institute rhapsodizes: "We have a self-perpetuating cycle, the key element of which is new paved roads. The 45,000 new miles added to the road and street network each year accommodate automotive travel, generate fuel consumption, produce road-building rev-

The open road these gentlemen enjoyed in their Packard in 1907 has become an insult to the sensibilities

enue." As A. Q. Mowbray comments in his illuminating and heartfelt *Road to Ruin* (1969): "It almost begins to sound like an argument for road-building as an end in itself."

"This vast program has developed a life of its own, an inherent bureaucratic momentum that seems almost unstoppable," says the *New York Times*. "The countryside is leveled and rolled and graded. The road-builders march—imperially, relentlessly, inexorably—across stream, meadow and woodland, through parks and nature preserves" as well as "through private homes, businesses and historic sites." For the damage does not stop with the city. From the start the juggernaut has zeroed in on the countryside, too.

There is, of course, the argument, to which the moguls of the industry never tire of resorting, that highways enable the populace to enjoy the beauties of the country. Obviously there is a great deal to this. In overwhelming degree, however, the scenic splendor that the highways provide is purely incidental. The aim of conventional highways is to connect communities along their routes; of freeways, to shorten the driving time between cities. Neither seeks any but the most grudging accommodation to terrain. Only the older roads do better, and they only in default of modern power equipment and appropriations back when they were built. To drive the highways of America is undeniably to have a great and exhilarating adventure much of the time. It is also to be crushed with discouragement over and over again. The charm and grandeur of the continent, which the motorcar brings us, are on a scale that has so far defeated even our civilization's assiduous efforts to destroy them, but they are conspicuously in retreat and in innumerable places in rout. The conventional highway brings with it a shoddy and clamorous commercialism that blights towns, villages, and countryside indiscriminately. Even "controlled-access" freeways are bordered by billboards in most states, thanks to the political influence of the outdoor advertising industry.

Federally aided highways were, of course, supposed to have been rescued from the blight of billboards and junkyards. That was one of the purposes of the Highway Beautification Act of 1965.

But, as the *New York Times* charged in 1969, the campaign "appears to stack up after four years as a failure." There is not enough steam behind it. "Of some 1.2 million signs on Interstate and primary highways, 839,000 of which were invalidated by the act, the Bureau [of Public Roads] knows of only 750 having been removed, with removal rights obtained on another 371." Progress in removing or concealing junkyards has been comparably poor. The Federal Aid Highway Act of 1968 provides that no state may require the removal of a billboard unless federal funds are avail-

every two of us. By the turn of the century more than 240,000,000 are expected, which will amount to one for every person and a quarter, or about one for every adult.

Moreover, the faster cars become, the more destructive are the highways needed to accommodate them. Every mile of today's Interstate freeway consumes about twenty-four acres; every interchange, about eighty. And for the extent of countryside this same freeway dominates without actually consuming, the figures could be multiplied by five or ten. Even at the lower figure the In-

some two hundred officials, engineers, and contractors from a dozen countries came to admire it, some from as far away as Australia and Indonesia. They were guests of International Harvester, which was showing how its big machines could gouge out a mountainside. For less than four miles of highway the government was spending 10.4 million dollars. But bad as that may sound, one mile of proposed freeway through Washington's Potomac Park, with tunnels, will cost seventy million dollars.

Thirty years from now there will be three hundred million of us in those

arge parts of the land. Above, left to right: Boston at rush hour; "Your Tax Dollars at Work" dissecting a California suburb; concrete spaghetti à la Atlanta.

able to compensate the billboard owners and then authorizes a paltry two million dollars for the purpose to take care of all fifty states! And now, even in states that prohibit billboards within 660 feet of the Interstates, industry is thumbing its nose at regulations by the erection of monster billboards outside the protected zone.

And what of the future? The Federal Highway Administration predicts that the annual national expenditure for highways and streets (now 8.5 billion dollars) will almost double after 1973. We can expect the mileage of new roads and streets (now 45,000 a year) to keep going up. Motorcars are even outmultiplying people in the United States. Ten years ago there were seventy million registered motor vehicles, or about one for every 2.4 Americans. Today there are one hundred million, or nearly one for

terstate freeways will dominate an area equal to that of Maryland and Rhode Island combined. (The area paved over thus far for the nation's roads equals that of West Virginia.)

The Bureau of Public Roads' statement that the excavations required for the Interstate System "will move enough material to bury Connecticut kneedeep in dirt" gives a suggestion of the damage to the country—and that is for a network of freeways considered sufficient only until 1975. Where the terrain is steep and apt to be most scenic the havoc is greatest. Whole mountainsides are sheared off and valleys filled with rubble. This is how the trucking industry, prime mover behind the Interstate System, likes it—since trucks find steep grades troublesome. Putting Interstate 61 around Clifton Forge, Virginia, for example, has involved destruction on such a scale that

more than 240,000,000 motor vehicles. Our disposable real incomes will probably be at least 50 per cent greater than at present, and we shall probably have 50 per cent more leisure time. To help us spend both, all kinds of recreational facilities will doubtless have grown up with the new highways, ranging from snack bars and bowling alleys to supermarinas and the kind of resort the Walt Disney organization has in mind for Mineral King, in the Sierra Nevada Mountains—a 35.5-million-dollar alpine village with twenty-two ski lifts, skating rinks, heated swimming pools, and five acres of underground parking. In thirty years the country should be pretty well given over to man and his works, with little chance for anyone to get away from either.

While the motorcar eats up the countryside and guts the city, it is creating

107

an amalgam of the two that seems to combine their attractions and advantages but in fact offers neither. Modern suburbia, the endless spread of houses on individual lots served by shopping centers behind vast parking plazas, is the product of the motorcar and could not exist without it. And suburbia is not a phenomenon of the city's environs alone. Not only the two- and three-car family but the two-house family is becoming commonplace. Summer suburbs of cottages, mean or grand, are overspreading our seashores, lakesides, riversides, and mountains, impairing if not eradicating their character as well, parcelling up and enclosing what should be the national commons. Finally there is nomadic suburbia; according to *Business Week* one new single-family dwelling in two this year will be a mobile home.

Suburbia is the disintegration of the human community. As Christopher Alexander, architect and city planner, writes, its inhabitants, moved by a "pathological belief in individual families as self-sufficient units," occupy "a collection of isolated, disconnected islands." They build their lives on that which sets the family apart, on the little private grass patch with outdoor grill, the television set, the motorcar, and, increasingly, the powerboat. To the minimum degree are their lives shared with others and refreshed and fortified by intimate contacts with others—the loss of which, Alexander warns, "may break down human nature altogether."

That we have been witnessing the unravelling of civilization in America is hard to doubt. Surely if the process is to be reversed the city must be redeemed and restored. We may well give equal importance to saving the countryside, but evidently we need not weigh the claims of one against the other; they are clearly but two sides of a single coin. Rehabilitating the city and saving the countryside both require a halt to the hybridizing of the two. The word must be: let that which is city be city and that which is country be country. Let them interpenetrate (as in Washington, D.C., with its green corridors of Rock Creek and Glover-Archbold parks), but let them be real city and real country, not a characterless fusion of the two that is neither. It may be just possible to slow the advance of suburbia. What that de-

pends on is dethroning the motorcar as the power that establishes the pattern of American life.

Admittedly, that alone will not return the cities to health. If the cities are to be livable, we shall have to arrest the growth of population. We shall have to enhance the attractiveness of the smaller communities so that they can hold onto their inhabitants and even win some back. We shall have to resolve the multiplicity of jurisdictions that hamstring metropolitan government. The races must be reconciled to one another on one basis or another. But without drastic control of

the motorcar nothing else seems likely to serve.

Creating new cities from scratch in the open spaces may be called for; our urban conglomerations are certainly growing far too large. But unless the forces that wrecked the historic cities are restrained, the fiat cities will be wrecked just as surely. So will the urban-renewed cities. Apart from this, the prospect is that the cities will deteriorate faster than money will be appropriated for renewing them unless the middle classes, with their disposable and taxable incomes and their habit of responsibility, can be brought back. This is the key. But the way to do it—and I am persuaded the only way— is to rein in the agency that spoiled the city's attractiveness and facilitated their flight. The first step to this end would be ceasing to abet it: no more building of freeways and of their tributary arteries

that propagate swarms of commuter-motorists; no more thoroughfares carrying traffic through settled areas at sixty miles an hour.

So much for phase one. Phase two would be to ease the great majority of private cars and *all* internal-combustion engines off the city streets. That would be to make the city healthful and enjoyable once more, to restore the charm of open, car-free vistas, to clear the avenues for expeditious public transportation, to rebuild self-contained, vital neighborhoods, to bring life and people and warmth and color back to the streets,

Old values or the rights of individuals are seldom allowed to stand in the way of highway progress. Abov

and children on roller skates and bicycles; to re-create a *human* city. The automobile industry talks glowingly of producing a pollution-free gasoline engine by 1980, but that is not soon enough. In the meantime a graduated increase in taxation of cars registered in the city and in tolls on those entering would do the trick. If it left a scattering of private cars on the city streets along with electric taxicabs, good enough.

Phase three, to be concurrent, calls for swift, capacious agencies of mass transit: steam-driven buses and electric trains below, at, or above ground level. Maybe even streetcars! The city's now-clotted blood vessels would flow once more. A bus will carry up to eighty passengers in the space occupied by two conventional cars with 1.7 occupants each (the average number per commuter car in the nation's capital). And on unencumbered streets it will move them fast. It is estimated that trains of eight cars can comfortably carry thirty to forty thousand persons per hour past a given point; the New York subways have achieved sixty thousand. By contrast a lane of a freeway with maximum carrying capacity of two thousand cars per hour moves only 3.4 thousand persons per hour. In other words one rail line will do the work that ten lanes of freeway do. And if it is adequately equipped, it will deliver its passengers at their destinations unexhausted, unfrayed of nerves, and with newspapers read.

foot or fast public transportation, with an endless variety of cultural and commercial offerings—between that and the monotonous, car-ridden suburbs, then yes. For such a city—which is entirely possible—would be the place for the good life and for rearing children. The middle classes would come swarming back.

What would go for urban freeways under the plan would go for cross-country freeways as well. We would stop building them. With the 42,500-mile Interstate System we would quit. When it became clogged we could let the diehard motorists and shippers stay with it

of its benefactor. The beguiling little kingaroo that America adopted was the tin lizzie. Today, as Marquis Childs observes, the motor manufacturers and big oil companies, standing together, comprise "probably the most powerful economic-political bloc in the nation, and with the highway lobby a force that can move mountains, literally or figuratively." Represented in the lobby are the rubber companies, the producers of cement and asphalt, manufacturers of construction machinery, building contractors, and assorted interests that reap the uncounted billions that annually go into motor traffic and its infrastructure. (In 1968 cars and car parts alone took 6.21 dollars out of every one hundred spent by the American people. With motorcar sales running at about ten million a year, or well over thirty billion dollars, and an annual repair bill of 8.8 billion dollars, Americans are spending more *directly* on their cars—leaving out gasoline, oil, insurance, parking fees, etc., not to mention highway construction and repair—than on public education.) The lobby has vigorous spokesmen in state highway commissioners and in the U.S. Bureau of Public Roads and the Federal Highway Administration, and powerful friends in the House Public Works Committee, which, as a prime source of pork, congressmen are not eager to antagonize.

'ents of Tennessee protest in vain against oncoming bulldozers, and a Vermont farm is forever imprisoned.

Mass transit does more than move people expeditiously and, on their part, effortlessly. The more the role of the private motorcar is circumscribed and the greater the public dependence on mass transit, the closer to mass-transit routes the public will domicile itself and employers locate themselves. That is how density of population is achieved. And density is the objective. It is only through bringing people close together, as opposed to dispersing them, that the city *and* the country can be saved.

But would the measures proposed result in the return of the middle classes? Few persons who value their time will without good reason spend the equivalent of one full working day a week commuting. But beyond that, if the choice were between a car-free city with miles of diverse and lively streets to explore, with parkland compact or vast accessible by

and fight the traffic battle. Others would have an alternative at hand: railroads. Travellers who needed a car where they were going (and most would not) could rent one at the other end or take one with them (a practice that just might cure us of our addiction to cars the size of gunboats). When it comes to moving people —or freight—the railroads, like urban trains, are line for lane far more efficient than the highways. And could anyone with the interests of a livable America at heart fail to rejoice if the railroads won back much of the business they have lost to cars and trucks?

. . . But back to reality. In one of cartoonist Al Capp's weird realms the ruler adopts a cute little animal that the wise man at court warns in vain is a kingaroo. The beast grows mightily and in doing so develops a fearsome appetite, which at maturity it satisfies by making a meal

Twice in the past several years the "road gang" has conspicuously demonstrated its might. When in November, 1966, as a means of reducing federal expenses and inflationary pressures, the Johnson administration announced that 1.1 billion dollars of the Highway Trust Fund would be held back, the outrage of the road gang was such that within seven months the administration had backed down all the way and released the entire amount withheld. In 1968 the Federal Aid Highway Bill showed the House of Representatives to be securely in the pocket of the highway men. (Key congressman had received seventy-five thousand dollars from the trucking lobby, according to Drew Pearson.)

The House bill, said Kentucky's John Sherman Cooper of the Senate Public Works Committee, "was more anti-conservationist than any other bill I have seen come before this body. In at least three major sections, it attempted to

109

strike down legislation which had been enacted by Congress in an effort to protect the natural resources and beauty of this country"—one specifically to protect public parks. The retrogressive measures were largely eliminated by Senator Cooper's committee but not the highhanded provision commanding the District of Columbia, as if it were a felon before the bar, to commence work within thirty days on four new components of the freeway system "notwithstanding any other provisions of law, or any court decision or administration action to the contrary." The package includes the North Central Freeway, which will plough through the Negro section of Washington with ten lanes, and the Three Sisters Bridge, which will destroy irreplaceable parkland and desolate one of the loveliest vistas of the Potomac while aiming straight up Glover-Archbold Park.

As the *New York Times* declared, "Apart from this proposed desecration of the capital, these bridge and freeway provisions set a most dangerous precedent for every city in the nation. If Congress can pick routes and choose bridge sites in Washington, D.C., and get away with it, there is nothing to prevent Congress from dictating similar decisions in other cities."

That Congress *is* getting away with it is owing primarily to a lawgiver from Bowling Green, Kentucky, William H. Natcher, chairman of the House Appropriations Subcommittee on the District of Columbia and errand boy of the highway lobby, as the *New York Times* describes him. Natcher ruled that until work on the extended freeway program had proceeded "beyond recall" no funds would be released for the city's long-discussed subway, the only possible cure for its transportation ills. Senate Majority Leader Mike Mansfield said on the floor of the Senate that "there is one issue on which almost every resident of the District agrees: opposition to more freeways," and he thought it "inconceivable" that the proposed rapid-transit system "could be held hostage to more unwanted freeways." It was, though. The city council, with two members in tears, finally knuckled under in a session marked by near riot.

But does it matter what decisions we come to about the motorcar? With the motor-age interests able to bend newspapers, governors, congressmen, and the United States government like pipe cleaners, has anyone a chance against them? And if anyone had, could the national economy afford a retreat from the motorcar in view of all the productive capacity and jobs that have been created to supply it and its wants?

Were it left to me, I should answer in a statement to the motorcar and highway interests. "Gentlemen, you have been turning out toys for chicken feed," I should say. "Incidentally, you have been pushing your country toward ruin. We offer you a chance to do a man's job for real money and, incidentally, take on the most exciting piece of work man has ever set hand to. *We call on you to rebuild the nation.*" Addressing Detroit, architect Philip Johnson has said, "Now look, turn your aims around. You now want to build great cities, not make automobiles. As in World War II, when you served public ends so efficiently and built no pleasure cars, adapt your incredible know-how, your great management abilities, to this new task. Do it efficiently and beautifully. Here is 100 billion or so for the first two years. Give us an accounting when you have used it up."

Asking why we do not live in good cities, Philip Johnson replies that "it can only be that we do not wish to. . . . Everyone seems to like other things more. It is my thesis that we shall not get cities designed closer to our hearts' desire until the values of people change. . . . If I am right, we face a dismal future. Popular faiths change slowly, slowly." And popular faith in the motorcar seems to remain a consuming one.

Yet there are signs of a burgeoning resistance to the "tyranny of the motorcar"—the currency of that expression being one of them. Because "the resentment is so deep," Mayor John V. Lindsay has overruled the projected Lower Manhattan and Cross-Brooklyn expressways. In Cambridge, Massachusetts, opponents of the Inner Beltway around Boston are still managing to hold the line. So are opponents of the proposed freeway along San Francisco Bay. Citizens' groups are still fighting hard to kill Three Sisters Bridge. Most spectacularly, a prolonged battle to save New Orleans' historic Vieux Carré district from an elevated freeway has finally been won, with the freeway's *coup de grâce* having been delivered by a former road contractor, John A. Volpe, Secretary of Transportation.

The Nixon administration has sponsored legislation providing for the expenditure of ten billion dollars over the next twelve years to help cities build mass-transit systems. This would represent a very great advance over the annual pittance the federal government is at present putting out ($175,000,000 to pay only half the costs of mass-transit systems) but hosannahs are being reserved until it is known how much is actually to be committed.

In the contest with the motorcar we may be able to count on the assistance of one force that is strong enough to dethrone it. This the Washington *Post* anticipated when, after charging automobiles with killing passenger trains and urban transit systems, it predicted that "In time, automobiles will kill themselves since the nation's fleet is now large enough to fill the 41,000-mile Interstate highway system bumper to bumper and is growing each year by enough to fill a two-lane highway bumper to bumper from Washington to Los Angeles." Before that auto-da-fé takes place, however —if the expression may be forgiven— irreparable damage may have been done to society. The basic decisions may have to be made much sooner; within five years, if the forecast of a traffic expert in the nation's capital is sound, "every single city-center area of every big city will be absolutely choked with automobiles."

Meanwhile nature conservationists and urban redemptionists may recognize that a common foe gives them a common cause. Every additional dollar of tax on motor vehicles and their requisites (a fifty-cent-a-mile levy would be proportionate to the damage the motorcar does, a pharmacologist at Stanford, Robert H. Dreisbach, suggests), every additional dollar of appropriations for public transportation, every dollar withheld from highway construction—is a step toward a supportable and rewarding way of life in the future.

Charlton Ogburn, Jr., is now at work on The Continent in our Hands, *a first-person narrative of discovery of the country's natural splendors and of what he believes confronts them.*

THE ENVIRONMENT:

Notes on the continuing battle   By ELIZABETH N. LAYNE

A JOLT FOR HONEY HOLLOW

On the gently rolling hills of Bucks County in eastern Pennsylvania five high-tension towers up to 140 feet in height, carrying five hundred kilowatts of electricity to the urban centers of New Jersey and New York, will be set in a three-hundred-foot corridor cut through the carefully nurtured woods and fields of Honey Hollow watershed—a National Historic Landmark. The rich, productive soil of Honey Hollow's six hundred acres has been continuously farmed since early in the eighteenth century. Substantial fieldstone houses and barns of that period still stand among the trim contour-plowed strips of corn, hay, and barley, the wildlife hedges, the ponds and terraces that have been maintained ever since five farmers of Honey Hollow watershed joined forces in 1939 to demonstrate the then newly developed U. S. Soil Conservation Service practices.

No specific wording in the National Historic Landmark Act of 1966 provides protection to historic sites from urban renewal projects, highways, or power lines. What little muscle the act does contain applies only to projects involving a federal agency. But the Federal Power Commission, which would be the appropriate government arm in this case, has no jurisdiction over the routing of power lines. It would seem logical for the Philadelphia Electric Company to have used an already existing route through the township for its new line, but this would have meant condemnation of houses, which Pennsylvania law strictly forbids. So a line was drawn on a map, and it fell across Honey Hollow.

In the fall of 1968 the National Park Service repeatedly wrote Robert F. Gilkeson, president of the utility company, asking that no action be taken before a landmark-status study was completed. Its letters went unanswered. And on November 25 the company officially established a route through Honey Hollow and proceeded to quietly buy up a farm in the very center of the watershed. About the same time Dr. S. K. Stevens, head of the Interior Department's Ad-

visory Council on Historic Preservation, informed Philadelphia Electric that the watershed would definitely be put on the national register, Honey Hollow residents learned that the power-line route had been shifted downhill so that it now cut through the heart of the area in about the most damaging way possible, both physically and aesthetically.

Power company officials could not understand why Honey Hollow farmers would object to high-tension towers (like those above) in their fields and at the edge of the pond (top above).

Precisely why this was done is not clear. The company claimed only that it was in the interests of the corridor concept (some years earlier a natural-gas line had been laid along that route).

On August 4, 1969, the watershed was officially designated a national landmark, and Honey Hollow became one of only 797 properties singled out for this distinction. Such landmarks, writes Secretary of the Interior Hickel, "require Americans . . . to pause and consider whether that which they are about to build is truly of greater worth than that which they are about to destroy." The president of Philadelphia Electric paused long enough to write the National Park Service, stating that the route for the line had been very carefully selected.

Up to this point all the clout belonged to the utility, but now the watershed group gained a weapon. The Army Corps of Engineers, in the surprising role of conservationist supporters, held up the permit needed by the utility to bring its line across the Delaware River. Suddenly the company agreed to search for an alternate route on land outside the boundaries of the historic landmark. But when it proved impossible to get such a right-of-way through purchase, they were unwilling to start lengthy condemnation proceedings. However, through the efforts and generosity of people who live on the watershed and of the National Audubon Society, arrangements for a route through a corner of the landmark were worked out with the owner of property at the edge of the watershed, who decided he would as soon have the transmission line run across his property behind his house and get paid for it as have the towers cross Honey Hollow in front of his house and not get paid for it. The landowners of the watershed are now working to bring Honey Hollow into the public domain so that this rare rural landscape may be saved from further damage. The area is also threatened by a proposed highway. Although the residents are proud of their accomplishment, conservationists are outraged that a power line will cross even a corner of the historic landmark.

A RIVER TO RUN FREE

The Big South Fork of the Cumberland River rises in the wilderness of east Tennessee's Cumberland Plateau. Its clear swift waters winding northward to Kentucky through the soft sandstone of the plateau have cut one of the most handsome gorges east of the Mississippi. Below high, varicolored bluffs the river courses along a jumbled bed of gigantic lichen-covered boulders, a churning white foam where the rocks channel the river through narrow chutes, long pools of quiet water where the valley widens. It seems a miracle that this magnificent river, within 250 miles of more than twenty-three million people, has stayed so untouched along its thirty-one-mile length. No one lives within the gorge itself or along the crest, no roads parallel the river, and only a very few cross it.

Shooting Angel Falls on the Big South Fork

But ever since 1962 the Army Corps of Engineers has tried to gain congressional authorization to build a 200-million-dollar, 483-foot-high hydroelectric dam on the Big South Fork at Devils Jumps pass in Kentucky. The lake formed behind the dam would still the rapids and drown the house-high boulders for twenty-nine miles back along the South Fork and for many more miles of the river's handsome tributaries. Five times the dam was approved by the Senate; five times it was rejected by the House Public Works Committee. Only conflicting economic interests—private power against public power, coal interests against hydroelectric power—kept the South Fork wild. By 1968 the economics of hydroelectric dams made such projects more difficult to justify. Also, the Tennessee Citizens for Wilderness Planning had been formed by two prominent geneticists at the Oak Ridge laboratories in Tennessee, Doctors William and Liane Russell, a husband and wife team who are also white-water enthusiasts and regularly float the Big South Fork. Thanks to their skillful efforts, the unspoiled river began to come to public notice. A 1964 Bureau of Outdoor Recreation wild-river report that had been suppressed came to light. The report had concluded that "the highest and best uses of the resources of the Big South Fork . . . appear to be as a national wild river from both a public recreation and economic standpoint." In July, 1968, at the urging of Senator John Sherman Cooper of Kentucky, who had always championed the dam to help the depressed economy of the area, the Army engineers and the departments of Interior and Agriculture were asked to submit to Congress a joint study report of alternative uses for the river without recommending any one of them. The 137-page report transmitted this February considered six alternatives "feasible and appropriate," including designation as a national scenic river, a recreation area, a national forest, and a national park. The future of the Big South Fork need no longer be settled on the narrow basis of a single project. Conservationists hope a similar broad basis for action will be provided Congress in other resource-development projects. The luxury of leaving an unspoiled area unprotected is no longer ours.

THE ENGINEERS SIGN ON

Chemical engineers in Texas have joined the pollution fight with a local program so successful that the American Institute of Chemical Engineers is encouraging others throughout the country to follow their lead. In March, 1968, Dr. A. Roy Price, thirty-nine, who works for a pollution-abatement company in Houston, led the formation of a volunteer Pollution Solution Group of some forty chemical engineers. Eventually they were joined by mechanical and civil engineers and other technically trained people. Dr. Price had been stung to action by Dr. John McKetta, then dean of engineering at the University of Texas, who has been severely chastising engineers for not joining the battle to save the environment.

As part of its program of public service, the group focused on the mud-pie-like Buffalo Bayou, which flows through the center of downtown Houston. With little hope for a major reduction in silt flow into the bayou (although they pinpointed and helped correct one major discharge from a laundry), the engineers set out to find a technique to clean it up. Months of careful work, closely followed by an interested local press, led to discovery of a way to use the liquid waste (containing aluminum chloride) from a nearby chemical plant to settle the solids and leave the water crystalline. The group is seeking a demonstration grant from the Federal Water Pollution Control Administration to extend its cleanup of the bayou.

Nowadays, most meetings of the Institute of Chemical Engineers will find Dr. Price, with an exhibit and copies of the action manual he has prepared, helping to start other groups on a course of effective grass-roots action.

Eight workbooks designed to give laymen some of the scientific and technical background necessary for effective action in helping to solve environmental problems have been prepared by the Scientists' Institute for Public Information. The titles offered are: *Air Pollution, Water Pollution, Environmental Effects of Weapons Technology, Hunger, Nuclear Explosives in Peacetime, Pesticides, Environmental Costs of Electric Power, Environmental Education: 1970.* They may be ordered from the institute at 30 East 68th Street, New York, New York, 10021, at seventy-five cents each.

112

THE GOOSE ON
THE DUCK STAMP

Since the passage in 1934 of the Migratory Bird Hunting Stamp Act all waterfowl hunters in this country have been required each year to buy a "duck stamp." The painting above of two Ross's geese by National Park Service artist Edward Bierly is the winning design for this year's duck stamp, to go on sale July 1 in U. S. post offices. Few Americans have seen these small (mallard-sized), immaculate white geese, and relatively little is known about them. The birds winter in the valleys of California and each spring fly north to nesting grounds in Arctic Canada. In spite of persistent exploration, the location of those grounds remained a mystery for nearly two centuries. But on the last day of June, 1940, two officers of the Hudson's Bay Company who set out from the Perry River post (about seventy-five miles north of the Arctic Circle) to look for the elusive nesting sites, finally solved one of North America's last remaining ornithological riddles. Angus Gavin, one of the men on the trip, described the excitement of that discovery.

"... towards evening everything was ready, and with Donovan and myself sitting in the middle of the canoe like factors of old, the natives dipped their paddles and we were off on one of the most delightful and thrilling trips it has been my pleasure to encounter in the North. The weather was perfect; each bend of the river brought new thrills. Ducks were everywhere, and the constant singing of the small birds, coupled with the harsher notes of the cranes and the honking of the geese, made sweet music. In a little while the rapids became faster, longer and more frequent, until at last we came to one that proved to be about a mile long. After labouring up this we came to a mile or so of good water, and it was while we were on this calm stretch that the first Ross's goose was sighted in the early morning light, flying towards the lake that lay ahead of us. Any doubts as to whether the geese we were looking for would be there certainly vanished when he appeared. On entering the lake, we could see them flying all over ..."

Most of the world's population of Ross's geese, perhaps thirty thousand in all, winter at the Merced and Sacramento national wildlife refuges in central California. Revenues (nearly six million dollars were collected last year) from the sale of duck stamps to hunters are used to acquire land for such refuges.

BUT WHY, GEORGE?

Nineteen sixty-seven was the year of the "long, hot summer"; Detroit and Newark were in flames, and longtime journalist Robert Cahn of the *Christian Science Monitor*'s Washington bureau vigorously protested when editor DeWitt John took him off urban affairs to do a fifteen-part series on the national parks and the problems created by the pressure of increased use. But his editor insisted, and that August, Cahn and staff photographer Norman Matheny started on a nine-month, twenty-thousand-mile inspection tour of twenty major park areas. Robert Cahn, fifty-two, a quiet, purposeful man, has been a working journalist since the Seattle *Star* took him on as a sportswriter the year he graduated with a B.A. in journalism from the University of Seattle. Over the years he has worked in various parts of the country for *Life*, *Collier's*, the *Saturday Evening Post*, and others. So reluctant or not, Cahn meticulously laid the groundwork for his journeys to the national parks with extensive interviews on each park's special problems. George Hartzog, director of the National Park Service, recalls, "I have answered his persistent 'But why, George,' at breakfast, lunch, and dinner, in a pickup truck ... climbing through Indian ruins, on an airboat in the Everglades, and on the back seat of a taxi returning from a congressional hearing." All those "but why's" asked of hundreds of park officials, park users, and concerned citizens produced a series of articles that generated so much interest that more than two thousand people bothered to fill in and mail to the *Monitor* a long questionnaire, which ran as the final installment of the series. It was the largest public survey ever conducted on park affairs. (The Park Service was surprised to learn the great majority of people wanted the parks preserved even at the cost of personal sacrifice or limitations on park use.) When he got back to his Washington desk, Cahn asked to spend full time reporting on the environment.

He won a 1969 Pulitzer prize for the series, and since then his perceptive, in-depth reporting on environmental questions has won him four other distinguished awards.

In January of this year President Nixon appointed Cahn to the newly created three-man Council on Environmental Quality, headed by former Under Secretary of the Interior Russell Train, with Dr. Gordon J. F. MacDonald, a distinguished geophysicist and expert on oil pollution, the third member. The council is to advise and inform the President on the broad sweep of environmental conditions. The qualities that earned Robert Cahn his reputation as an outstanding reporter and analyst on environmental issues should now be of great service to the entire nation.

Robert Cahn

Letters to the Editor

FLIER'S IMP

Sir: The December article "A Flier's Journal," by General Kenney, was of special interest to me as the former Commanding Officer of the 2nd Photo Section assigned to the 91st Observation Squadron (I succeeded the Lieutenant Suydam who is mentioned).

Perhaps you might be interested to know the story behind the 91st insignia accompanying the article. This design was taken from the drawing used on the masthead of the editorial page of the old *Life* magazine and was adopted as their official insignia. This design was painted on each side of the squadron's planes, and for every German plane officially confirmed as being brought down by the pilot-observer crew, a black German cross was painted on the shield of their plane. Four or five crosses were not uncommon. . . .

William A. Barnhill
Gainesville, Florida

STRIP MINING: THREE STATES

Sir: . . . For years now newspapers and television documentaries have reported in horrifying detail that central Appalachia—and eastern Kentucky in particular—is being shredded by strip mining. [See AMERICAN HERITAGE, December, 1969.] The truth of this reporting has been verified by both state and federal studies. Multitudes of worried and compassionate people have visited the region and deplored the heartless assaults against the land and the men, women, and children who call it their home. Scores of politicians (including Lyndon Johnson and Robert Kennedy) have come to see the devastation and poverty, and editorial writers have used

barrels of ink denouncing the exploitation. But despite all the outrage and hand-wringing, the strip mining goes on. The trees continue to fall, the streams continue to die as valley after valley is gutted, and the impoverished and demoralized people continue to flee to Michigan and Illinois. Exposés and public outrage count for nothing against the money and prestige of the corporate destroyers. They are, apparently, too big and too rich to check.

For example, Kentucky appropriates no money to police strip miners. The companies pay fees for permits to dismember mountains, and if no permits are issued, no funds will be available to pay the salaries of enforcement officers. Consequently, a steady flow of licenses is guaranteed no matter how steep the terrain or beautiful the doomed forest. Strict enforcement would shrink and eventually destroy the Reclamation Commission, and no one who understands the nature of bureaucracy can suppose the agency will ever enforce its way into oblivion and joblessness.

Then, too, the commission is indecently cozy with the companies. In the fall of 1969 the Louisville *Courier-Journal* disclosed that Elmore Grim, the state's reclamation director, was permitting his office to be used to wring political contributions from the operators. . . .

The operators naturally have few fears after their money flows to the state's capital, and such conventional "rights" as freedom of the press can be safely trampled by them and their hirelings in and out of public office. When Miss Jean Martin, a photographer for Whitesburg's *Mountain Eagle*, sought to make pictures of land stripped for Bethlehem Steel she was attacked, her film was forcibly taken, and her life was threatened . . .

Here in Pike County we wait in vain for an answer to our letter to the president of Bethlehem asking for information as to their plans for stripping the mountains above our homes. For two years we have been asking Bethlehem to clean up the mess they left as a result of previous mining operations, and for two years our requests have been met with indifference and contempt. . . .

Tom Ramsay
Director
Pike County Citizens Association
Hellier, Kentucky

Sir: . . . To show that strip mining need not ruin the landscape, you might take a look at Pennsylvania. To my knowledge this is the only state that requires complete restoration of coal-stripping operations. Since the passage of our bituminous strip-mine law in 1963 coal operators have had to restore their operations to original contour concurrent with mining, prevent the discharge of acid water, and *successfully* plant the restored land.

These requirements are being carried out on mountain slopes as well as on rolling farmland. Our experience is that total restoration is both economically and technically feasible. The law is strongly enforced. . . .

Fred Jones
Conservation Editor
Pittsburgh *Press*
Pittsburgh, Pennsylvania

Sir: . . . In southern and central Illinois, for example, a "New Land" program has long been sponsored by the United Electric Coal Companies, now a subsidiary of General Dynamics. Since 1938 U.E.C. has actively sought to improve the land from which coal has been extracted. Today, there are some eighteen thousand acres of New Land with forests, pastures, orchards, and over two hundred lakes. Some of the areas are wildlife preserves for deer, quail, rabbits, beaver, and wild game. Others are grazing ground for cattle or forests for future timber. The orchards produce twenty-seven thousand bushels of apples as well as a crop of peaches. . . .

Typical of the New Land policy has been reforestation. Recognizing the need for a timber crop that could be harvested within a man's lifetime, seedlings of southern pine were imported. Despite criticism that the area was too cold and rocky and the competition from the native hardwoods too severe, these pines today are seeding themselves and helping to create attractive lake and forest areas. . . .

One of the major reasons for the success of this reclamation program is the manner of mining. U.E.C. was the first coal company to develop the wheel type of excavator. This removes the overburden by digging upward so that the dirt and shale are deposited on the land in such a way that the earth can be regraded and easily planted.

Coal is still the most important commodity around a strip-mine area. But after the coal is gone, the New Land remains with ever-increasing abundance and opportunity for recreation. . . .

Paul Seastrom
Land Manager
The United Electric Coal Companies
Du Quoin, Illinois

EARLIEST FACE?

Sir: Recently, in the course of some research for a book, I arrived at a conclusion which I would like to expose to your readers. It requires a brief explanation:

Sometime in 1844 or 1845, on a trip up the Hudson to photograph Martin Van Buren and Washington Irving for his "Gallery of Illustrious Americans," Mathew Brady paid a call on Major John Livingston, veteran of the Revolutionary War and a member of the distinguished Livingston family (his brother Robert was an author of the Declaration of Independence; Chancellor of New York State; the Minister to France who negotiated the Louisiana Purchase; and patron of Robert Fulton, who named his steamboat *Clermont* for the Livingston estate). Brady's daguerreotype of Major Livingston was made when the old gentleman was in his ninety-first year (he was born in 1755, the year of Braddock's defeat, and lived until 1851).

I believe that this extraordinary daguerreotype shows us the likeness of a man who was born before any other American of whom we have a photograph. Indeed, it is possible that Major Livingston antedates *anyone* whose photograph survives.

COLLECTION OF RADFORD B. CURDY

Major John Livingston

It would be interesting to know if any of your readers have information indicating that a photographic likeness exists of anyone born earlier than 1755.

Richard M. Ketchum

Mr. Ketchum, Managing Director of the American Heritage Book Division and author of several books, has completed a book, Faces from the Past, *based on the familiar series of that name in these pages. It has just been published by the American Heritage Press.*

IRONSIDES INDEED

Sir: "Old Ironsides" lived up to her name during the hurricane that hit New England in 1938. ["A Memorandum to Oliver Wendell Holmes," February, 1970].

As the daughter of a naval officer living in the Boston Navy Yard, I remember my father being called out during the height of the storm. Old Ironsides' stern lines had parted. Her stern swung over and dented the then new, all steel destroyer U.S.S. *Phelps*, tied up at an adjacent dock. As I recall, there was not a scratch on the old *Constitution!* . . .

She is priceless and must be preserved.

Jean Kell Steer
Athens, Georgia

VANISHING FOREST

Sir: Having received a ballot for the American Heritage Society Awards to preservation projects, we wish to commend your organization on the remarkable foresight and concern shown for our vanishing environment and historical heritage.

We certainly hope that the leadership shown by publications such as yours in providing not only space but also money for citizen groups struggling to reverse the current destructive trends will generate a real awakening in this country.

The Thorn Creek Preservation Association is a group involved in an attempt to preserve the last sizable undeveloped forest in a three-hundred-square-mile area south of Chicago in eastern Will County, Illinois. It is directly in the path of urban growth, and part is included in the plans of a new community. A new university is to be built adjacent to the site, Chicago's third airport can possibly go near here, and an east-west freeway is proposed to run through the forest.

There is a change in the climate of public opinion on environmental problems, due in a large measure to the responsible leadership of the news media. If the elected officials can only catch up to the public demand, perhaps there will be some hope for projects such as ours. . . .

Marvin Harr
Chairman
Thorn Creek Preservation Association
Richton Park, Illinois

FAUNTLEROY LANDMARK

Sir: The February feature "A Wrecker's Dozen" included a photo of the Franklin School of Washington, D.C., slated for demolition. It is an interesting coincidence that this school was the alma mater of Vivian Burnett, "The Real Little Lord Fauntleroy," who was the subject of my article in the same issue. Vivian and his brother, Lionel, both attended Franklin School. They were together in the eighth grade at the school with Miss Ella Morgan as their teacher when "Fauntleroy's" brother was stricken with his fatal illness.

Tom McCarthy
Goshen, New Hampshire

Letters to the Editor CONTINUED

MOUNT MONADNOCK REVISITED

Sir: Nine years ago, in the December, 1960, issue of AMERICAN HERITAGE, at the close of a spread on stereopticon slides, you printed a picture of Mount Monadnock. Since that time we have had a desire to see if we could find the exact spot that the picture was taken from. Last week we had an opportunity and spent some four hours cruising the roads west of the mountain with the pictures in hand, checking and comparing views.

As you can see from the accompanying photographs, we were successful. The area has grown up so much that it is no longer possible to see the mountain clearly, but a number of the rocks in the stone wall can be identified, particularly two in the lower left-hand corner of the AMERICAN HERITAGE picture. Our photograph was taken from a spot probably no more than six feet from where Mr. French set up his tripod. The spot is in the township of Marlboro, New Hampshire, on the Old Dublin Road, about 150 yards northeast of its junction with the Old Monadnock Road. By walking about one hundred yards to the left down the road we found a clearing from which we could see Monadnock clearly. All four of the trees visible in the picture can be found in the woods, now hoary old sugar maples. . . .

All this classifies as useless information, but we were interested, and we thought that you might be too. At one point during our search we were stopped by two men who thought that we looked like burglars preparing to rob some of the summer houses in the area.

> Richard V. Upjohn
> Seaver R. Gilcreast, Jr.
> Fay School
> Southboro, Massachusetts

We congratulate Messrs. Upjohn and Gilcreast for their perseverance; the New England back country is often a tangle of old stone walls that run right through the woods. Once they separated fields and meadows of hardscrabble Yankee farms, but now they disappear into the second growth that has been rising for the century and more since the farmers went away forever to pioneer in the West. —Ed.

COLLECTION OF LORRAINE LETHURAY DEXTER

116